IN SEARCH OF YOUR GERMAN ROOTS

GERMANY

★ State Capital   ☐ Over 1 million
⊛ Federal Capital   ☐ Over 500,000
◉ Federal Government   ● Over 100,000
◇ Supreme Court(s)   • Over 50,000

© 1994, Geosys Company

DENMARK

Baltic Sea

Flensburg

Kiel ★

Schleswig-Holstein

Stralsund

Rügen

● Rostock

Lübeck ●

Schwerin ★

Mecklenburg-Western Pomerania

North Sea

(Nth.-Bd.)

Wilhelmshaven ●

Bremerhaven (Bremen)

Hamburg

Hamburg

Luneburg •

Schwedt •

POLAND

Oldenburg ●

⊞ Bremen

NETHERLANDS

Lower Saxony

⊞ Hannover

Stendal •

Potsdam ★

⊞ Berlin ◇

Brandenburg

Osnabruck ●

● Hildesheim

Magdeburg ★

Munster ● ● Bielefeld

Dessau •

Cottbus ●

North Rhine-Westphalia

Paderborn •

Gottingen ●

Saxon-Anhalt

Essen ■ ■ Dortmund

Halle ●

■ Leipzig

Dresden ★

⊞ Dusseldorf

Kassel ●

Erfurt ★

Jena ★

Saxony

Görlitz •

Neuss •

Siegen •

Gera ●

Chemnitz ●

Aachen •

■ Cologne

• Marburg

Thüringia

Zwikau •

Bonn ◉

Hesse

Fulda •

Suhl •

Plauen •

BEL.

Koblenz •

Weisbaden ★

Frankfurt ■

Schweinfurt •

Hof •

CZECH REPUBLIC

LUX.

Rhineland-Palatinate

Mainz ★

Darmstadt •

Würzburg ●

Bamberg •

• Trier

Saarland

Ludwigshafen • Mannhiem

Heilbronn •

Nüremberg ●

Saarbrucken ★

⊞ Stuttgart

Ingolstadt ●

Regensburg ●

Bavaria

Karlsruhe ◇

Baden-Württemberg

Ulm •

Augsburg ●

Landshut •

FRANCE

• Freiburg

⊞ MUNICH ◇

• Rosenhein

AUSTRIA

Konstanz •

• Kempten

SWITZERLAND

LIECH.

Angus Baxter

In Search of Your German Roots

A COMPLETE GUIDE TO TRACING YOUR ANCESTORS IN THE GERMANIC AREAS OF EUROPE

Fifth Edition

GENEALOGICAL PUBLISHING COMPANY

First Edition © 1987 by Angus Baxter
Second Edition ("United Germany Edition") © 1991 by Angus Baxter
Third Edition © 1994 by Angus Baxter
Fourth Edition © 2001 by Angus Baxter
Fourth Edition, Updated © 2008 by Susan Baxter

Published by Genealogical Publishing Company
3600 Clipper Mill Road, Suite 260
Baltimore, MD 21211-1953
www.genealogical.com

Library of Congress Catalogue Card Number 2014959057
International Standard Book Number 978-0-8063-2011-3

Made in the United States of America

Dedication to the Fifth Edition

All my life I have known exactly where I come from; not just the town of my birth, but the roots and lives of my ancestors. I know the roads they walked, the fields they farmed, and the sheep they sold at market. I have even seen the houses where some of them lived. This is entirely because of my father, Angus Baxter, and his passion for genealogy. The contentment it has brought me is beyond measure. I am so lucky to have had the parents I did. My father loved life and he loved his family. My mother, my daughter, and I all basked in this love. Thank you, Daddy. I miss you.

Susan Baxter

CONTENTS

INTRODUCTION

When this book was first written in 1987, searching for German ancestors was a more cumbersome and likely a more expensive proposition. A lot of legwork was required in order to pinpoint what records were available in Germany and where they were housed, letters had to be written and fees paid, followed up by weeks of waiting for responses. The LDS Church had begun their ongoing project to copy records of genealogical value in Germany, but they may not have gotten around yet to copying the particular records you required. Now, almost thirty years later, millions more birth, baptism, death, and burial records; civil registrations; censuses; and archival collections have been copied, indexed, and made available at no cost through LDS family history centers and online at **https://familysearch.org**.

There have been many other developments in recent years that have made German family history research immeasurably easier, including the following (to name just a few):

- The roll-out of Archivportal-D, a free Internet portal that enables users to access millions of data sets from upwards of 25 participating archives and view general information on another 400 institutions.
- Kirchenbuchportal, a new Internet portal for German church records.
- The availability online of Jewish records from Landesarchiv Baden-Wuerttemberg—a collection that previously could only be viewed by making a trip to Stuttgart.
- Matricula, an Internet site that is beginning to place digitized German and Austrian religious records online.
- Online access to approximately 2,000 historic German-language newspapers.
- Easier access to vital records in Germany due to a change in privacy laws.
- Websites now available for all the major archives and most of the smaller ones and church parishes in Germany, containing contact information, descriptions of holdings, and frequently, searchable databases and online images of records.

All of the above and much more are discussed in this fifth edition of *In Search of Your German Roots.*

This book is written to help you trace your ancestors in the "old country"—whether your German forebears came from Germany or Austria or one of the many European countries that had German settlements. It will give you only a little information about records on this side of the Atlantic because there are many books available on this subject. Of course, I will talk about major areas of German settlement in North America, such as Pennsylvania and the Midwest, and the Kitchener area of Canada.

Why should you bother to trace your ancestors—those unknown men and women who created you? What benefits will you obtain from your search?

There are no easy answers to these questions but your place in the scheme of things will be more secure. You will know more about yourself and the members of your family who preceded you. When you start to search for your German ancestors you will be setting out on a journey of the heart and mind that will bring you happiness and romance beyond all measure.

No one can say for sure why, all over the world, men and women are searching for their roots. Some, perhaps, hope to find a missing family fortune, a title of nobility held in abeyance until a claimant comes along, or a family coat of arms. However, I believe the answer is quite a simple one—we, or our children, simply want to know where our family originated and what our ancestors were like.

We want to know what they did, how they earned a living. Why did they leave home to cross the Atlantic? What was happening in their country at that moment in history? What clothes did they wear? What food did they eat? These are our questions, and we are the people who will answer them if we are patient and determined.

As you travel back through the years you will acquire no financial rewards—most family stories of missing fortunes are without any foundation—but, on the other hand, you will not have to spend a great deal of money. Of course, you can pay professional researchers to do your work for you, but this is totally unnecessary. Genealogy is a do-it-yourself hobby, and this book is designed to help you do just that. Researchers will probably bring you results, but however good they are, they will lack your great personal advantage—your love of your family.

You will need other assets, of course—an organized mind and the patience and determination I mentioned above. You may encounter many obstacles and dead ends.

You will need to know your history, because the great and remarkable race from which you are so proudly descended has spread across the continent of Europe. Great events of history have changed frontiers, created new countries, destroyed old ones, and through all these cataclysms the German race has left its mark in many areas far beyond the borders of what we now call Germany.

Because you have a German surname and a family story that "great-grandfather came from Germany," do not assume that he came from that area of Europe marked "Germany" on the map. He could have come from Austria, Belgium, the former Czechoslovakia, Denmark, France, Italy, Liechtenstein, Poland, Romania, Switzerland, the former USSR (including the Baltic states of Estonia, Latvia, and Lithuania), or the former Yugoslavia. All these countries are either German-speaking or have large German minorities. The Germans in these countries kept their own customs, their religion, their ancestral pride, and their records. Their passion for order is a priceless legacy for you.

You can do much of your searching by e-mail correspondence and exploring the Internet, by working in your own home at your own pace, by using the resources of libraries and archives or church and government records. You do not need to visit the place from which your family came to this country—although one day your own natural curiosity may take you there. Resist the temptation to board a plane tomorrow. You will accomplish much more by sitting down and reading this book—keeping it beside you as you search.

As your work progresses you will be in touch with people in the old country—priests and ministers, archivists and librarians, friendly civil servants (yes, they do exist!), and genealogical and historical organizations. You will be making contacts and friends—and maybe even distant cousins who will welcome you when you do go overseas. By then, too, you will have learned a great deal about your forebears; you will be able to walk the fields they plowed, worship in the churches they attended, visit the houses in which they lived, and you will not be a stranger in a strange land.

As you turn the pages of this book you will learn about the history of the German people; you will find out what resources are available; and you will find out where to locate these sources of information.

Don't take on too much research at a time. Start with just one side of your family; otherwise you will only become confused with the dozens of names you will collect as time goes by. "Was that Ernst Müller or Ernst Brand? Was it Anna Frank who came from Munich (München), or was that Anna Fiedler?" You will also find that when you are searching long lists of names it will be much easier to look for one surname than seven or eight. Of course, if two or more sides of your family came from the same village, that is quite a different story—you will save time and money by looking for them simultaneously.

With the passage of time your family tree will grow, and as it does you will find out many things about the people who made you. You will find answers to questions you have often asked, and to questions you have never known you wanted to ask. You may even discover physical appearances and traits of character that will tell you why you are as you are.

Finally, you must be warned that in your search, as you go further back in the records, you will be confronted with the old Germanic script. In its printed form it is not too difficult to grasp because it resembles the script used on the title page of many newspapers—*The New York Times*, for example. It is in its handwritten form that the real problems arise. A further complication is that the earlier church records were often written in Latin. I suggest you try to take the free online German Script Tutorial on the FamilySearch website (**https://familysearch.org/learningcenter/ lesson/german-script-tutorial/91**) or try to locate a copy of *If I Can You Can Decipher Germanic Records*, by Edna M. Bentz. It was privately published in San Diego in 1982 (reprint 2006). It not only explains and illustrates Germanic script but also lists handwritten examples of many of the words you will encounter in your own research—emigrant, sponsor, sergeant, innkeeper, lessee, miner, farmer, priest, settler, and so on.

Enough of these preliminary words of wisdom! With the aid of this book you are starting on an exciting voyage, and no one knows where it will take you or what treasures you will find along the way. Perhaps there really was a castle on the Rhine once owned by your family— maybe an ancestor stood on the battlements of Marksburg and watched the ships sail slowly by on the river far below. All this lies ahead with the discoveries you will make as you search for your German roots.

All addresses, phone numbers, URLs, e-mail addresses, etc., have been updated and were correct at the time of publication. The international telephone and fax numbers that appear in this book have been presented in such a way that readers may call from the United States.

Be aware that URLs, addresses, and contact information can change. If you find a URL or address that is no longer accurate, do an Internet search for that organization to locate its new contact information.

While preparing the various editions of this book, I was helped by many kindly and co-operative people. There are too many people to mention all of them, but there are some I must thank by name: Thomas Schmid, Fr. Regina Mittner, Dr. Udo Hahn, Dr. Peter Vorster, and Dr. H. Wentner.

Publisher's Note: Since Angus Baxter's passing in 2005, Genealogical Publishing Company has kept many of his titles in print and in updated form. As Mr. Baxter's United States publisher, we would like to acknowledge the unfailing support of his daughter, Susan Baxter, in this ongoing endeavor. Most recently, this new fifth edition of *In Search of Your German Roots* was completely updated and revised by Marian Hoffman. It is due to her thorough and diligent work that this invaluable research tool will continue to provide guidance for genealogy researchers well into the twenty-first century.

CHAPTER 1:
STARTING THE SEARCH

Start with you and with no one else. Do not take someone with your surname who was famous two centuries ago and try and trace his or her descendants down to you. First, it is impossible and, second, there is little likelihood of a family connection anyway.

Having said that, surnames can sometimes help you identify your ancestors' place of origin, a crucial piece of knowledge for beginning your family history research. For example, certain surname suffixes are associated with specific geographical areas—in northwestern Germany you'll find names with suffixes such as –sen (Dirksen), -sohn (Mendelssohn), and –s (Carstens), all meaning "son of," while the suffix –en (Otten) is found in East Frisian areas, and a name ending with –ke comes from northern Germany. Typical Swiss endings are –i and –y and prefixes Zum and Zur. You can find German and Austrian surname distribution maps at **http://christoph.stoepel.net/geogen/en/Default.aspx**.

Names, however, can be misleading in four ways:

1. Even within a few generations of a family, the spelling of a name can change. Usually this was because, with a few exceptions, our ancestors could not read and write and so the name would be spelled phonetically (as it sounded). There was, in fact, a double complication, for the name could sound different to different people. The spelling changes could occur on different occasions— when your ancestor was arranging with the local clergyman for a baptism, a marriage, or a burial; when he was registering with the local police for an internal passport; when he was answering the questions of the census enumerator; when he was registering for compulsory military service; when he was booking passage on a ship; or even when a name was being carved on a tombstone. In my own family records you will find Baxter, Backster, Bagster, Bacaster, Bacster, Bakster, Bacchuster—even Bastar (I didn't like

that one very much!). In Germany, for example, Meyer can be spelled as Mayer, Meier, Meir, Mier, or Maier.

2. Don't assume that everyone with the same name as yours must be related to you somewhere back in time. Up until the fourteenth century (and much later in some parts of Europe) there were no surnames. People were known by their first name, and attached to it was a word describing where they lived or what they did, or even an event such as a flood that took place when they were born. So a man named Wilhelm might be Wilhelm from the wood (Wald), or Wilhelm the baker (Bäcker), or Wilhelm the wagonmaker (Wagner), or Wilhelm born in the storm (Sturm). Sometimes, too, a newcomer to a village would be known, for example, as Wilhelm from Erlangen (this would be written as Wilhelm von Erlangen, so I am sorry to say a "von" in your ancestral name does not necessarily mean your forebears were noblemen!). By about 1400 the population growth and increasing movement of the population made the lack of a surname a nuisance, and so the "the" or "of" or "from" was dropped.

3. You may find your surname was changed a couple of generations back. This could have happened for several reasons—your ancestor may have decided his name was too long or too complicated for use in a new country and so he might have made it shorter; or he may have decided to anglicize his name so that Schmidt became Smith; or he might have encountered an immigration officer who said, "Rosenkrantz? What sort of name is that? I'll put you down as Rose."

4. In certain areas, particularly in Holstein and Ostfriesland, the system of patronymics was used (giving children a surname based on their father's first name), so that Peter Bergmann could have a son with the name of Wilhelm Peters. In some cases, too, a man might have a surname based on the name of his farm, and if he moved to another farm his surname would change. However, patronymics and farm names are not always a problem because usually the real family name was entered afterward in parentheses as "sonst" (meaning otherwise) or "angenommener" (meaning adopted).

Make a list of all known living members of your family, including even the most distant cousins, with their contact information, if known. Once this is done you can start to ask questions—in person, on the phone, and by e-mail or snail mail. Write down everything you are told and be sure you also write down the name of the person who gave you the information—you may need to query an item with that person later on.

If by any chance you have elderly relatives, this may be like striking the mother lode. They might well know when and where people were born or died, and who married whom. Remember, too, that they can tell you not only about the events of their own lives, but also about events they heard of from their grandparents. In the clear mind of an elderly person you may find 150 years of family history—a rich source of material just waiting to be uncovered.

Ask everyone about everything you need to know—date of arrival in this country, name of the ship, port of arrival, occupation, religion, place of origin, place of death, place of burial, military service, date of naturalization—some of this information you will have already, some you will need to search hard for, but it will all help you along the road. So far as religion is concerned, a word of caution: Coming from Germany, your family will probably be either Catholic or Evangelical Lutheran. Remember that people can change their religion—either through marriage, conversion, or happenstance. The latter could occur if your deeply religious ancestor settled in a place in this country where there was no Lutheran church. There might have been a Methodist chapel, and so he might have decided to attend services there. When a Lutheran church was built he would have reverted to his original denomination, but for a period of several years the vital events of the family may have been recorded in the Methodist church registers.

I mentioned earlier the importance of talking to every member of your family. Just one member may have information unknown to anyone else. Let me tell you a story. My wife was born in Scotland and so were her parents and grandparents and several generations beyond them. When she was a small child her grandfather mentioned to her that the family had come from England 200 years before. She remembered this, and many years later she commented about the story to her father. He told her there could not be any truth in it—the family was Scots way back forever (you must understand that if you are Scots and have English blood in your veins, you keep quiet about it!).

When we started to trace my wife's family back, we remembered grandfather's story and, without going into all the details, we found he was right to within twenty years. What is more, we traced the man who came from England and found a published family tree in a history book, which took us back to 1680 and gave us clues that eventually took us back to 1296. All because one member of a family was told something vital.

So some family stories are true, but many are not, and all stories should be treated with caution until you have proof as to their truth.

Quite apart from contacting family members and friends, you must also search for family records of all kinds—letters, diaries, naturaliza-tion papers, family Bibles, family photograph albums, etc. A word of warning, though, about family Bibles. It was fashionable up until about 1900 to present one to a newly married couple so they could record the vital events of the new family—births and baptisms, and, eventually, marriages and deaths and burials. Special pages were provided for such records, either at the front of the Bible or between the Old and New Testaments. Often, people starting to trace their ancestors accept all the handwritten entries as "gospel," but "it ain't necessarily so," as Gershwin put it. If all the entries are in the same handwriting with no variation in style and neatness over more than two generations, the odds are that many entries were made long after the event and are, therefore, based on "hearsay" and are not reliable without other confirmation.

The family photograph album you possess is probably the most frustrating record you will find. There are all those lovely pictures of solemn-looking men and women who must be ancestors—but, unfortunately, no one has written their names below the photograph or on the back. Possibly your elderly relative can help to identify some of them for you. However, there is one clue in the album that may be of value to you. The chances are that the name and city of the photographer of any studio pictures will be printed or embossed on the front or back of them. If this same city is repeated several times, it is quite likely to be the place from which your immigrant ancestor came. He may have brought some of the photos with him, or they may have been sent out by the family he left behind—"Here is a photograph of your brother Heinrich and his new wife, Elisabeth." You can also use this clue of a possible place of origin in two other ways—first, to check if someone has already traced your family and, second, to try to find relatives still living in Europe.

This is what you must do:

1. *Has someone already traced your family back?*

There are a number of databases available on the Internet containing information on millions of surnames. You can find many of these listed at **www.cyndislist.com**, by typing your surname into a search engine, or by visiting the largest genealogical community on the Internet—**Ancestry. com** (Ancestry.de for the German version). You can also check out the following organizations to see if they have any record of the family:

(a) Visit the FamilySearch website of The Church of Jesus Christ of Latter-day Saints (the LDS Church) at **https://familysearch. org** or visit one of their family history centers worldwide. FamilySearch holds the largest collection of genealogical material in the world. This is described in detail in Chapter 3.

(b) Contact or visit the public library of the place in this country where your ancestor settled, and the library in the place from which he came (or you think he came). Contact the national, provincial, and local archives in the particular area in Europe. Get in touch with genealogical societies and family history societies in the same area. In all these cases explain what you are doing and give as much information as you can about the sailing date, date of arrival in this country, place of settlement, religion, and occupation.

(c) Post a query on a message board such as the German Genealogy Forum (**http://genforum.genealogy.com/germany/**). Ancestry. com has message boards for all of the German states, as well as one covering all of Germany.

It would be a major tragedy if you were to spend a couple of years and, perhaps, a couple of hundred dollars tracing back your forebears, only to discover the search had already been made and you had never checked! Let me give you an example of what may happen. Some years ago my wife and I decided to trace her grandmother's side of the family in Scotland—the name was Copland. We already had the information for four generations back, but beyond that all we knew was that the family had been living in the area of a city named Dumfries, in the southwest of Scotland. We were in the country at that time on a visit, and so we went to Dumfries prepared to spend a couple of weeks there visiting churchyards, churches, and so on. First of all, though, we went to the local library, met the librarian, and asked him, "Do you, by any chance, have information about a family named Copland that used to be prominent in this area a century and a half ago?" "Oh, yes," he replied. "I have a great deal of information about the family." He then produced a 400-page typed history of the family written by a family member fifty years earlier!

It was complete in every detail. The author had done his research most thoroughly and had meticulously recorded the source of all his information. Within thirty minutes we had found just where my wife's branch of the family fitted into the family history. From then on, all the work had been done and there was a complete record of the family— documented and proved—back to a man named Ulf the Viking, Lord of Copeland, who had been alive in 1135. This took my wife's ancestry back twenty-four generations! If we had not checked with the library, it would have taken us several years to go back that far. We also found that we were twenty-second cousins, or something like that, since I am descended from that same Viking through my Curwen ancestors.

2. *How do you find out if you have living relatives in Europe?* Of course, you try to find this out from within your own family, but if you fail to discover anything, then there are two methods to use:

(a) If you know or believe your ancestor came from a particular small city or town or village, send an e-mail or write a brief letter to the local newspaper. If your ancestor came from a big city like Berlin, Munich, or Vienna, the big dailies are unlikely to publish it—small-town or county papers will nearly always do so.

(b) If you don't know the name of the local newspaper, it doesn't matter. Try an Internet search or simply write to Der Redakteur, Die Zeitung, Nürnberg (or whatever is the name of the town or area in which you are interested). Your letter should be short and on the following lines:

> My great-grandfather, Alois Furst, emigrated from your area in 1890. He was a farm worker. His father was named Johann. If there are any relatives still living in Nürnberg, I would very much like to hear from them.

(c) Another possible source of information is the telephone directory. Many international telephone directories are now available online. For example, complete German telephone directories—with numbers for archives, individuals, and businesses—are available at **www.gelbeseiten.de/**, **www.yalwa.de/**, and **www. dastelefonbuch.de/**. If you have an uncommon German name, you can contact the embassy or nearest consulate of Germany, or whichever country is involved, and ask if they would be kind enough to photocopy the page in the local phone book for the place or area in which you are interested. If your name is Muller, forget it! If it is Klippenhoffer, then try it! The name must be uncommon, otherwise the method is not practical. Once you have your list of names and addresses—hopefully about twenty or thirty—then you can send a letter to the first five. If it brings no results, then write to the next five, and so on. Be sure to include your e-mail address so that people can reply to you that way. Here again, be brief and say:

> I saw your name in the phone book. My great-grandfather, Alois Furst, emigrated from your area in 1890. His father was named Johann. If you are descended from his brothers or sisters, or are in any way related to him, I would very much like to hear from you.

This is as good a place as any to talk about language. Of course, it is better if you can write all your inquiries in German—to archives, to libraries, to churches, to newspapers, and to names in a phone book. However, if you have lost your ancestral language, try and get your e-mails or letters translated by a family friend who speaks the language, by a local high school teacher, or by the local German society or organization. If all else fails, it is better to write in good English than in bad German.

You will probably get responses from people who are not related but are complete strangers going out of their way to help you. People all over the world are, generally speaking, kind and friendly—it is the other kind, unfortunately, who hit the headlines! Let me give you an example of what may happen to you—it happened to me.

My family originated in a remote valley in the Lake District of England. I traced them back in a proven and continuous line to 1340, and from then with gaps to 1195. A number of years ago I wrote a letter to the *Westmorland Gazette* (the local paper) asking if, by any chance, a reader had photographs of the houses and farms in which my ancestors had lived (I listed them) and, if so, could they lend me prints to be copied, or have them copied in England at my expense.

I had three replies from people who did not have any photographs but who had made special journeys to the valley to photograph the houses for me. One couple even made a short movie of the valley for me.

I mentioned above that you should contact family history societies for information as to whether anyone has already traced, or is tracing, your family. You should also give some thought to becoming a member of the organization covering the district from whence your ancestors came, providing that you are not experiencing language problems. There are several good reasons for joining such a society:

1. It publishes a newsletter at regular intervals, and you will obtain a great deal of information about the area and its genealogical records.
2. It will keep you up-to-date as to new sources of information, and old ones that have just reappeared after many missing years.
3. It will publish your queries in the newsletter or online free of charge.
4. It lists the names and addresses of members and the names for which they are searching.

If you are interested in Germans from the Palatinate there is a society, and if you are interested in Germans from Prussia there is a society for that area too. Many of these are listed later on in this book.

There were important changes in the German Postal Code system after the unification of East and West Germany. Before unification the postal codes for each location had the prefix O or W to distinguish between East and West Germany. All numbers were four-digit. Now there is a five-digit code applicable to the whole country. It is very important that you use the postal code because of the duplication of place-names in the country. There are, for example, a dozen places named Königsberg! Some of them are tiny villages.

CHAPTER 2:
THE GERMANS AND GERMANY

If we think about our German ancestry, it is easy to be led astray by lack of knowledge of the original Germanic tribes and their descendants. Without this knowledge it is difficult to avoid making mistakes that may delay or even halt forever our search for our German roots.

When we read about German colonies, we only find mention of Tanganyika, Southwest Africa, the Cameroons, and Western Samoa, but over many centuries the hardy and adventurous German race has, in fact, colonized many parts of Europe.

A number of different tribes formed the German race more than a thousand years ago—Franks, Bavarians, Saxons, and Swabians, to mention only a few of them. Today, German is the mother tongue of 100 million people.

The development and coalescence of the German nation took many centuries. The word "Deutsch" (German) was first used in the eighth century, but it only referred to the spoken language of the area known as eastern Franconia. This empire reached its height of importance under the Emperor Charlemagne (Karl der Grosse), and after his death in 814 it disintegrated. The western section eventually became the area we now know as France. The eastern section varied in area over the centuries, but the main area—the heartland—became known as the Deutschland (the land of the Germans). By 911 the Duke of Franconia was elected King of the Franks, and later King of the Romans. By the eleventh century the area became known as the Roman Empire, and by the thirteenth the Holy Roman Empire. In the fifteenth century the words "German Nation" were added.

Before and during all these dynastic and political events, the German tribes overran most of the original Roman Empire as far east as the Elbe—beyond it were the fierce Slavic tribes. During this period the tribes took firm root in what we now know as Switzerland, Liechtenstein, Austria, northern Italy, the Netherlands, and the Baltic states. They were also invited into Transylvania by the Hungarian king in 1150. Siebenburgen—the German name for Transylvania—derives from the seven fortified towns established by the Germans. Although they came from the Rhine and Moselle area, they were known as "Saxons." There were some 5,000 settlers who were given as much land as they could cultivate and allowed to retain their own customs and language. Some did not stay long but moved south into the area known as the Banat, or west into Hungary proper. After eight centuries their descendants are still in Transylvania. However, there are now only some half-million of them, since the rest fled to Germany when the Communists took over after the Second World War.

While all this was going on, the Order of the Teutonic Knights and the Livonian Brothers of the Sword were extending German power into the Baltic countries of Estonia, Latvia, and Lithuania. The Teutonic Knights were formed originally to take part in the Crusades but eventually settled in Prussia in 1309, and then extended their power and influence eastward into Livonia and Courland. At the same time King Andrew II of Hungary called on the Teutonic Knights to protect Transylvania from the Cumans and the Mongols in the east. So both northeastern and southeastern Europe were "colonized" by the Germans. The prime aim of the Knights was conquest and loot, but behind them came settlers, bringing a predominant German influence into the conquered territories. The Drive to the East (Drang nach Osten) started with Charlemagne's armies and the Teutonic Knights, and ended with Hitler.

During this period there were also smaller migrations to Schlesien (Silesia), which is now divided between the Czech Republic and Poland, and to Bessarabia—until 1945 Romanian and now largely in Moldova. In the reign of the empress Maria Theresa of Austria (1740–1780), many Germans—the so-called Danubian Swabians—migrated to four areas of Hungary: Bacska, the Banat, the Kingdom of Croatia, and part of Slovakia. A number of these settlers later moved on into Ukraine, Bessarabia, and other areas of southern Russia. Others—like the Zipsers—settled in Slovakia.

After the First Partition of Poland in 1772, Frederick the Great of Prussia (1740–1786) settled West Prussia and the area around Bromberg with German emigrants from Württemberg and Baden-Durlach. Said the king, "Get me farmers from Württemberg and the economic misery will come to an end."

In the middle of the eighteenth century, the empress Catherine the Great of Russia (1762–1796) invited all foreigners who possessed skills of some kind to come to her country as settlers and colonists. In cases of financial hardship, the cost of transportation was paid. In addition, all settlers received a loan of money toward the cost of building a house and buying livestock and farm or trade equipment—with repayment required in ten years.

The proclamation of the empress was distributed throughout Europe but did not meet with any great response except in the Germanic area and, to a much smaller degree, Sweden. Most of the colonists came from Hesse (Hessen) and the Rhineland, but all German-speaking areas were represented in varying numbers.

I must quote to you the titles of the empress as set out in her proclamation. No, it will not help your genealogical research one little bit, but I found it amusing and so, I hope, will you:

> Empress and Autocrat of all the Russians at Moscow, Kiev, Vladimir, Novgorod, Czarina of Kazan, Czarina of Astrachan, Czarina of Siberia, Lady of Plaskow, Grand Duchess of Smolensko, Duchess of Estonia and Livland, Carelia, Twer, Yogoria, Permia, Viatka, and Bulgaria and others; Lady and Grand Duchess of Novgorod in the Netherland of Chernigov, Resan, Rostov, Yaroslav, Belooseria, Udoria, Obdoria, Condonia, and Ruler of the entire North Region and Lady of the Yurish, of the Cartalinian and Grusinian czars, and the Cabardinian land, of the Cherkessian and Gorisian princes, and the lady of the manor and sovereign of many others.

The areas opened up for settlement by the empress were underpopulated and open to frequent attacks by the Ottoman Turks. The Germans, for their part, were eager to settle for a variety of reasons. Germany as we know it today did not exist. It was a vast conglomeration of 1789 kingdoms, principalities, grand duchies, dukedoms, electorates, free states, and free cities—down to tiny independent states of a few hectares. Men were dragged off into various warring armies, women and children were raped or killed or both, agriculture was ruined by the constant wars, and people starved. There was also religious persecution, as well as high taxes, civil disturbances, and in many areas a high population density. Life was miserable and dangerous for the ordinary people, and it was no wonder the grass in the next field looked much greener.

If your family is descended from the Germans who immigrated to Russia between the mid-1700s and the mid-1800s, you may have assumed there is no chance of tracing your forebears back to their place of origin in the area that is now Germany. In fact, there is a very good chance records exist that will give you vital information.

Between 1804 and 1842 over 72,000 people immigrated to Russia, and estimates for the entire period range as high as 150,000 from the German area alone. It was one of the great mass movements of history. For a century they poured into Russia and established themselves in fairly close areas of settlement in the Volga region, the Black Sea area, and the Caucasus.

The whole story is documented in a remarkable two-volume work by a very remarkable man—Dr. Karl Stumpp. It is entitled *The Emigration from Germany to Russia 1763–1862* and was published by the American Historical Society of Germans from Russia (AHSGR), 631 D Street, Lincoln, NE 68502 (phone: 402-474-3363; e-mail: ahsgr@ahsgr.org; website: www.ahsgr.org). It is now also available on CD and lists the names of some 50,000 German settlers, with their places of origin and settlement.

It may be helpful to quote the areas of origin and settlement over the century:

Period of Emigration	Place of Origin	Area of Settlement
1763–68	Hessen, Rheinland, Pfalz, Sachsen, Württemberg, Switzerland	Volga (E and L)
1765	Sulzfeld, Württemberg	Reibensdorf (E)
1766	Hessen, Württemberg, Brandenburg	Petersburg, Black Sea
1766	Hessen	Belowesh (E and C)
1780	Preussen, Württemberg, Bayern	Josefstal, Fischerdorf, Jamburg, in Dnieper area
1782	Sweden	Schwedendorf (E)
1786	Preussen	Alt-Danzig
1789–90	Danzig, West Preussen	Chortitza (M)
1804–6	Alsace, Pfalz, Baden	Franzfeld, Mariental, Josefstal, by Odessa (C)
1804–6	Württemberg, Alsace, Pfalz, Baden, Hungary	Grossliebental, Neuburg, Alexanderhilf
1804–6	Danzig, West Preussen	Halbstadt, Molotschna (M)
1804–6	Württemberg, Baden, Hessen	Prischib, Molotschna (E and C)
1804–6	Württemberg, Switzerland	Neusatz, Zürichtal, in the Crimea (E and C)
1808–10	Württemberg, Alsace, Pfalz	Bergdorf, Glückstal, Kassel, Neudorf, by Odessa (E)
1808–10	Alsace, Baden, Poland	Baden, Elsass, Kandel, Selz, Mannheim, Strassburg (C)
1808–10	Alsace, Baden, Pfalz, Württemberg	Beresan and Odessa (C)
1812–27	Württemberg, Baden, Hessen	Prischib, Molotschna (E)
1814–16	Württemberg, Preussen, Bayern, and Poland	Bessarabia, and near Odessa
1817–18	Württemberg	South Caucasus (E)
1821–34	Württemberg, Preussen, Bayern, and Poland	Bessarabia, and near Odessa

Period of Emigration	Place of Origin	Area of Settlement
1822–31	Württemberg	Swabian colonies near Berdjansk (E)
1823–42	Danzig, West Preussen, Baden, Hessen, Rheinland	Grunau area (E and C)
1853 and 1859–62	Danzig, West Preussen	Samara (M)
	(This was the last emigration from Germany)	

(E=Evangelical, L=Lutheran, C=Catholic, M=Mennonite)

When the German armies invaded the USSR in 1941, they were welcomed by the majority of the Germans living in Ukraine. When the Wehrmacht retreated in 1942 many of the German settlers left too, fearing reprisals from the Red Army, and they were wise. They made their way back to Germany, the fatherland their ancestors had left more than a century before, and those left behind in Ukraine were killed or imprisoned.

Millions of Germans in other areas of Europe became refugees after the Second World War. In 1945 Czechoslovakia regained the Sudetenland. This German-speaking area had been taken from Austria in 1919. In 1938 it was reunited with Germany. After 1945 the three-and-a-half million German inhabitants were expelled and their property and possessions confiscated. Other refugees from Poland and the USSR brought the total number of Germans returning home to over thirteen million.

Quite apart from the mass movements of population shown above, there was, of course, a continual movement to and fro between the multitude of German states before and after unification in 1871. Most of these movements of individuals were recorded, and the records are in the various state archives. If a man wished to move from Hannover to Brunswick, for example, he would notify the Hannover police of his impending departure and his destination. On arrival in Brunswick he had to report to the police within three days. They, in turn, notified the Hannover police that he had arrived.

Although these tremendous upheavals will have a major effect on your ancestor-hunting, you must also become aware of other problems ahead. For example, there are large numbers of Germans still in Denmark, Belgium, and Alsace (Elsass), and many German speakers in the South Tirol—now in Italy.

In addition, you must consider the "lost territories" of Germany and what has happened to their genealogical records. These territories consist of the following areas:

To Belgium: In 1919 Eupen, Malmédy, and Moresnet
To Czechoslovakia: In 1945 the western part of Silesia (Schlesien)
To Denmark: In 1920 North Schleswig

To France: In 1919 Alsace (Elsass)

To Poland: In 1945 the eastern parts of Brandenburg, Pomerania (Pommern), the southern part of East Prussia (Ostpreussen), Posen, the western part of Silesia (Schlesien), West Prussia (Westpreussen), and Danzig

To the USSR: In 1945 the northern part of East Prussia (Ostpreussen) and Memel

The genealogical records for these areas are located in the various archives listed below:

Belgium: Church and civil records of the transferred area are in the State Archives at Liège (Archives de l'État à Liège, Rue du chéra 79, 4000 Liège; e-mail: Archives.Liege@arch.be; website: http://arch.arch.be/). A number of inventories of the State Archives in Liège are available online (**http://arch.arch.be/content/view/1104/312/lang,en_GB/**).

Czech Republic: The two major cities from Silesia now in this country are Leitmeritz (now Litoměřice) and Troppau (now Opava). The addresses of the two archives are as follows:

Státní oblastní archiv v Litoměřicích (State Regional Archives Litomerice); Krajská 48/1, 41201 Litoměřice; e-mail: info@soalitomerice. cz; website: www.soalitomerice.cz/. North Bohemian vital records housed at the archives are searchable online at **www.soalitomerice.cz/ en/content/vital-records-search.**

Zemský archiv v Opavě; Sněmovní 1 746 22 Opava; e-mail: podatelna@ zao.archives.cz; website: www.archives.cz/. A number of online databases containing records of interest to genealogists are searchable at **www.archives.cz/zao/digitalni_archiv/index.html.**

Denmark: The old Duchy of Schleswig-Holstein was divided in 1920. The northern part went to Denmark and the southern part remained German. Records for the latter part are in the Landesarchiv Schleswig-Holstein (Prinzenpalais, 24837 Schleswig, Germany; e-mail: landesarchiv@ la.landsh.de; website: www.landesarchiv.schleswig-holstein.de/).

The census records for the area lost by Germany are located in the Landsarkivet for Sønderjylland (Haderslevvej 45, 6200 Aabenraa, Denmark; e-mail: mailbox@laa.sa.dk; website: www.sa.dk/laa/). The church records for the northern part are also in these archives, as are copies of some of the Holstein records.

France: For information regarding Alsace-Lorraine contact the following archives:

Archives départementales du Bas-Rhin (6, rue Philippe Dollinger, 67000 Strasbourg; e-mail: archives@cg67.fr; website: http://archives.bas-rhin.

fr). The Archives' vital records are now available online. They include parish registers from the 16th century to 1792; 10-year index and civil registers of birth, marriage, and death from 1793 to 1912; family names' choice registers by Jews (1808).

Archives départementales du Haut-Rhin (3, rue Fleischhauer, 68026 Colmar Cedex; e-mail: archives@cg68.fr; website: www.archives.cg68. fr/. The Archives' Internet site allows you to search their collections and several databases.

Service départemental d'Archives de la Moselle (1, allée du Château à Saint-Julien-lès-Metz, B.P. 25260, 57076 Metz Cedex 3; e-mail: archives@cg57.fr; website: www.archives57.com/).

The Department of Moselle is in the process of putting online the registers of the Catholic and Protestant parishes from villages located in the departmental territory, as well as records of the Jewish community of Metz in the 18th century.

Poland: After World War II as many as one million ethnic Germans living in Poland were naturalized and granted Polish citizenship. Today, there are an estimated 350,000 ethnic Germans still living in Poland, the majority of which live in the southwestern Polish region of Silesia (an area of Poland that formed part of Germany until 1945).

Poland is divided into counties (voivods), and each has its own archives. Those of the following cities and the area around them may be helpful in your search. The original German name is given first and then the new Polish name and address are in parentheses. Mail inquiries should be sent to Archiwum Państwowe, followed by the street address, postal code, and the city or town name in Polish:

Allenstein (ul. Partyzantów 18, 10-521 Olsztyn); e-mail: sekretariat@ olsztyn.ap.gov.pl; website: www.olsztyn.ap.gov.pl

Breslau (ul. Pomorska 2, 50-215 Wrocław); e-mail: sekretariat@ap.wroc. pl; website: www.ap.wroc.pl

Bromberg (ul. Dworcowa 65, 85-009 Bydgoszcz); e-mail: dz.info@ archiwum.bydgoszcz.pl; website: www.bydgoszcz.ap.gov.pl

Danzig (Walowa 5, Pomorskie, 80-958 Gdańsk); e-mail: apgda@gdansk. ap.gov.pl; website: www.gdansk.ap.gov.pl

Grünberg (AL. Wojska Polskiego 67A, 65-762 Zielona Góra); e-mail: sekretariat@archiwum.zgora.pl; website: www.archiwum.zgora.pl

Kattowitz (ul. Józefowska 104, 40-145 Katowice); e-mail: kancelaria@ katowice.ap.gov.pl; website: http://katowice.ap.gov.pl

Köslin (ul. Marii Skłodowskiej-Curie 2, 75-803 Koszalin); e-mail: secretariat@koszalin.ap.gov.pl; website: www.koszalin.ap.gov.pl

Oppeln (ul. Zamkowa 2, 45-016 Opole); e-mail: sekretariat@opole. ap.gov.pl; website: www.opole.ap.gov.pl

Pless (ul. Brama Wybrańców 1, 43-200 Pszczyna) (branch of the Katowice archives); e-mail: appszczyna@katowice.ap.gov.pl; website: www. katowice.ap.gov.pl

Posen (ul. 23 Lutego 41/43, 60-967 Poznań); e-mail: archiwum@poznan. ap.gov.pl; website: www.poznan.ap.gov.pl

Schneidemühl (ul. ppłk Aleksandra Kity 5, 64-920 Piła) (branch of the Poznań archives); e-mail: pila@poznan.ap.gov.pl; website: www. poznan.ap.gov.pl

Stettin (ul. Św. Wojciecha 13, 70-410 Szczecin); e-mail: sekretariat@ szczecin.ap.gov.pl; website: www.szczecin.ap.gov.pl

Thorn (Plac Rapackiego 4, 87-100 Toruń); e-mail: archiwum@torun. ap.gov.pl; website: www.torun.ap.gov.pl

You can check the availability of parish and civil records housed at the various Polish State Archives online at **http://baza.archiwa.gov.pl/ sezam/pradziad.php?l=en.**

Russia and the Former USSR: Some church and civil records do exist for former areas of Germany or German settlements. The State Committee on Archives in Ukraine has a good website called "Archives of Ukraine" at **www.archives.gov.ua/Eng**, which gives tips on accessing archives, genealogy research, and online resources. In addition, the Russian State Historical Archive (RGIA) in St. Petersburg contains many records of Germans who did business or worked in Tsarist Russia, were included in Russia because of boundary changes, or immigrated to Russia as colonists. The Archive was closed for two years while it relocated to a new state-of-the-art building in 2008 (check their website at **www.fgurgia.ru** for information about their holdings).

There are some records of genealogical interest in the National Archives in Washington, D.C., including the following:

Records of the Reich Commissioner for the Baltic States 1941–45 (Microfilm T 459, rolls 3, 11, and 12).

Records of the Reich Ministry for the Occupied Eastern Territories 1921–45 (Microfilm T 454, rolls 1, 2, 3, 16, and 107).

These two series were microfilmed by the U.S. government at the end of World War II and contain details about archives in the Baltic States and Belarus. They include the records of the Civil Registry Offices (ZAGS) and a number of parish registers. There are no indexes to these records. The originals are in the Landeshautarchiv Koblenz, Karmeliterstrasse 1-3, 56068 Koblenz, Germany (**www.landeshauptarchiv.de/**).

Two other websites that may be of some help are ArcheoBiblioBase's "Archives in Russia" at **www.iisg.nl/abb/**, which lets you search the archives of federal, regional, and local archives in Russia; and "Archives of Belarus" at **http://archives.gov.by/eng/**, which contains extensive information on the various archives in Belarus.

The state archives in the Baltic states of Estonia, Latvia, and Lithuania also contain Lutheran and Catholic Church registers as well as civil registration records from 1919. The addresses of the archives are given below.

Estonia. The State Archives are located at Maneeži 4, 15019 Tallinn (e-mail: rahvusarhiiv@ra.ee; website: www.riigi.arhiiv.ee/). The Estonian Historical Archives (J. Liivi 4, 50409 Tartu; e-mail: rahvusarhiiv@ra.ee; website: www.eha.ee) holds records of churches, educational institutions, and manors, as well as personal files. You can find information about both of the above archives on the website of the National Archives at **www.ra.ee.** Searchable databases of Estonian family history archival sources are available online at **www.eha.ee/saaga.**

Latvia. There are three state archives in this country. The Latvia State Historical Archives (Slokas iela 16, 1048 Rīga; e-mail: vestures.arhivs@arhivi.gov.lv; website: www.arhivi.lv/index.php?&110) holds records of the pre-Soviet period. The State Archives (Bezdelīgu iela 1, 1048 Rīga; e-mail: lva@arhivi.gov.lv; website: www.itl.rtu.lv/LVA) has records of the Soviet occupation period. The State Archive of Audiovisual Documents (Šmerļa iela 5, 1006 Rīga; e-mail: aed@arhivi.gov.lv; website: www.arhivi.lv/index.php?&421) is also of interest to genealogists.

Lithuania. The state archives in Lithuania of interest to genealogists include the following two archives: the Central State Archives (Lietuvos centrinio valstybės archyvo, O. Milašiaus 21, LT 10102, Vilnius; e-mail: lcva@archyvai.lt; website: www.archyvai.lt/en/archives/centralarchives.html), which has birth, marriage, and death registers, wills, and land records; and the State Historical Archives (Lietuvos valstybės istorijos archyvas, Gerosios Vilties 10, LT 03134 Vilnius; e-mail istorijos.archyvas@lvia.lt; website: www.archyvai.lt/en/archives/historicalarchives.html), which has vital records of the different religious communities.

Germany only existed as an undivided country from 1871 until 1945—in contrast with England and France, which had been unified for more than five centuries. Systems of government in the various German states ranged from absolute monarchies to the near-democracy of some of the electorates and free cities. Various forms of confederation or economic grouping took hold, flowered for a few years, and died. Each state had its own laws, archives, and system of recording events. You cannot say, for example, that "censuses were first held in Germany in 1871." That is true for the unified Germany, but censuses were taken in Württemberg in 1821, in Baden in 1852, and so on. The only unified force in the Germanic area was the church—first the Catholic and later the Lutheran.

By the middle of the nineteenth century, the number of self-governing German states had been reduced to thirty-four. Some of these formed the German Confederation, which also included Austria—still trying to assert its position as leader of the German people. However, the alliance was a shaky one because of the emerging power of Prussia, under the leadership of the great Bismarck. The two rivals did join together in an attack on Denmark in 1866 and seized Schleswig-Holstein, which they divided between them. A few months later they quarreled over the "spoils," and Prussia took over the whole territory. At this point Austria withdrew from the German Confederation and joined with Hungary in 1867 to form the Austro-Hungarian Empire.

The German Confederation was then renamed the North German Confederation under the leadership of Prussia, and included all the states north of the River Main. The eastern boundary was extended as far as Memel. In 1871, following a short and successful war against France, Prussia persuaded the southern states to join the Confederation with its new name of German Empire (Deutsches Reich). The king of Prussia was then proclaimed emperor on January 16, 1871. Suddenly, in the very center of Europe, a most powerful new country existed, and for the first time in over a thousand years the German people were one nation under strong leadership.

In the short period of a quarter of a century, the German people had developed a pride in their nation, which was strong enough to overcome the hatreds and mistrusts of a thousand years of division and despair.

The new empire included the following territory:

(a) Kingdoms of Bavaria, Prussia, Saxony, and Württemberg;
(b) Grand Duchy of Baden;
(c) Free Cities of Bremen, Hamburg, and Lübeck, and Anhalt, Brunswick, Darmstadt, Hesse, Lippe, Mecklenburg, Oldenburg, Reuss, and the various states comprising Thuringia. (Justice, education, health, and police were left under the control of the individual states.)

During the period of unification between 1871 and 1945, little or no attempt was made to centralize records in one place, such as the capital, Berlin. Instead, they remained in the capital cities of the original states. In retrospect, this was a blessing to ancestor-hunters because the destruction of German records during the Second World War was surprisingly small. Imagine what would have happened if everything had been in Berlin!

Details have already been given of the post-war dismemberment of Germany and the transfer of territory to Czechoslovakia, Poland, and the USSR. The remaining part of Germany was then divided into the eastern half, occupied by the USSR, and the western half, occupied by Britain, Belgium, France, and the United States. These two parts later became the German Democratic Republic (Deutsche Demokratische Republik, or D.D.R.) and the Federal Republic of Germany (Bundesrepublik Deutschland, or B.R.D.). Details of the division were as follows:

D.D.R.: Anhalt, Brandenburg (western part), part of Brunswick (Braunschweig), Mecklenburg-Schwerin, Mecklenburg-Strelitz, Reuss, Sachsen-Altenburg, Sachsen-Meiningen, Sachsen-Weimar, Schwarzburg-Rudolstadt, and Schwarzburg-Sondershausen. Also four provinces of the State of Prussia (the parts remaining after territory taken by the three countries mentioned above).

B.R.D.: Baden, Bavaria (Bayern), part of Brunswick (Braunschweig), Coburg, Lippe, Oldenburg, Schaumberg-Lippe, part of Thuringia (Thüringen), Waldeck, Westphalia (Westfalen), and Württemberg; and five provinces of the State of Prussia—Hanover (Hannover), Hessen-Nassau, Rhineland (Rheinland), Schleswig-Holstein, and Sigmaringen.

After the division of Germany in 1945 various changes were made in each section of the country, and they were administered as follows:

D.D.R.: Originally this consisted of five provinces (Länder). These were abolished and replaced by fifteen districts (Kreise). However, the D.D.R., unlike the B.R.D., was not a federal state, and all power was centered in the capital (East, or Ost, Berlin).

B.R.D.: Originally this consisted of ten federal states (Bundesländer, or just Länder): Baden-Württemberg, Bavaria (Bayern), Bremen (city-state), Hamburg (city-state), Hesse (Hessen), Lower Saxony (Niedersachsen), North Rhine-Westphalia (Nordrhein-Westfalen), Rhineland-Palatinate (Rheinland-Pfalz), Saarland, and Schleswig-Holstein. The city-state of Berlin (West) was integrated into the legal and economic system of the Federal Republic. The republic was further divided into twenty-five administrative areas (Regierungsbezirke), 327 counties or districts (Kreise), and about 8,500 municipalities.

The sixteen states of the unified country and their capital cities are:

Baden-Württemberg (Stuttgart)
Bayern (Munich/München)
Berlin (Berlin)
Brandenburg (Potsdam)*
Bremen (Bremen)
Hamburg (Hamburg)
Hessen (Wiesbaden)
Mecklenburg-Vorpommern (Schwerin)*
Niedersachsen (Hannover)

Nordrhein-Westfalen (Düsseldorf)
Rheinland-Pfalz (Mainz)
Saarland (Saarbrücken)
Sachsen (Dresden)*
Sachsen-Anhalt (Magdeburg)*
Schleswig-Holstein (Kiel)
Thüringen (Erfurt)*

The Länder marked with an asterisk (*) are the political divisions of the area previously known as East Germany. They replace the fifteen districts (Bezirkes) mentioned on the previous page. The names of the districts within each of the five Länder are:

BRANDENBURG: Berlin, Cottbus, Frankfurt, Potsdam
MECKLENBURG-VORPOMMERN: Neubrandenburg, Rostock, Schwerin
SACHSEN: Dresden, Chemnitz (formerly Karl-Marx-Stadt), Leipzig
SACHSEN-ANHALT: Halle, Magdeburg
THÜRINGEN: Erfurt, Gera, Suhl

THE CONTINUING MIGRATION

Earlier in this book I wrote about the great Germanic migrations in the Middle Ages and in the eighteenth and nineteenth centuries. After World War II approximately thirteen million Germans left their homes in other European countries and found refuge in the Fatherland. Since the unification of Germany and free emigration from the former Soviet Union and Eastern Europe, there has been a huge influx of ethnic Germans.

The Germans in Kazakhstan numbered nearly a million at the time of the Soviet collapse—some descended from the Germans who originally settled in the Volga Basin at the invitation of Catherine the Great, and others who were exiled from Ukraine by Stalin. Most have migrated since then, usually back to Germany or to Russia. There are now an estimated 180,000 ethnic Germans remaining in Kazakhstan.

CHAPTER 3:
THE RECORDS
OF FAMILYSEARCH

Anyone starting to trace his or her German ancestors should make use of the nonprofit family history organization operated by The Church of Jesus Christ of Latter-day Saints (the LDS Church), FamilySearch, which has the largest collection of genealogical and historical records in the world. If you are tracing your German ancestors, FamilySearch's records may be very valuable to you.

The interest of LDS church members in genealogy stems from their theological belief that family relationships and family associations are intended to be eternal and not limited to a short period of mortal existence. Church members "sealed together" are not married only "until death do you part." It is believed that a husband and wife and their children remain together throughout eternity as a family unit with their ancestors and descendants.

Members of the church collect genealogical information about their ancestors in order to perform "sealing ceremonies" in temples erected for that purpose. Before the sealing of families from generation to generation can be performed, the families must be properly identified. This is done by members' own personal research and by using the records of the church—in particular the extraordinary collection of the Family History Library (located at 35 North West Temple, Salt Lake City, UT 84150; phone: 866-406-1830) and the vast amount of digital information now available online at **https://familysearch.org**.

FamilySearch is engaged in the most comprehensive genealogical research program ever known. Microfilming and computerization are at the heart of the operation, and every day genealogical records in more than 100 countries are being copied, filmed, and preserved on microfilm and compact discs (CDs), and in computers. Documents such as parish registers, censuses, civil registrations, land records, probate records and wills, marriage bonds, funeral sermons, military rosters, guild membership lists, school attendance records, cemetery records, and passenger lists have all been copied. Records—the majority of which contain information about persons who lived before 1930—are available from the United States, Canada, the British Isles, Europe, Latin America, Asia, and Africa.

There are several ways that you can consult this massive collection of records. You can visit the Family History Library in Salt Lake City, stop at one of the 4,745 branch family history centers operating throughout the world (check **https://familysearch.org/locations/** to find the location of the nearest family history center), or utilize the FamilySearch website (**https://familysearch.org**). If you want to look through the registers of the Evangelical Church of Hohenfriedeberg in Silesia (Schlesien), Grabau in Posen (Poznań), or Stallupönen in East Prussia (Ostpreussen); or get a list of everyone named Bernheim in the Evangelical Church registers of Dortmund between 1710 and 1915; or get information about Gerhard Eichler who was a goldsmith in Köln in 1785; or locate details of the next of kin who was a Feldwebel (sergeant) in the 18th Hussars in Vienna (Wien) in 1848—you can do all these things.

The FamilySearch website offers free access to digital images of historical genealogical records and numerous databases. These include birth and baptism records, death and burial records, marriage records, city records, military records, and much more; go to **https://familysearch. org/search/collection/list#page=1&countryId=1927074** for a list of the FamilySearch Historical Records Collection for Germany.

The Records search page on the FamilySearch website lets you enter the name of the person you are researching and then narrow your search to a specific locality—or a specific type of record—in your country, state, or province of interest. You can also go to **https://familysearch. org/learn/wiki/en/Main_Page** and type in a specific locality or topic of interest (e.g., Schleswig-Holstein parish records) to find out what records are available for that topic.

You can consult the FamilySearch Catalog—previously known as the Family History Library Catalog—at **https://familysearch.org/catalog-search** for Germany-related genealogical materials (including books and other publications, online materials, microfilm, and microfiche) made available by FamilySearch. Many of these items can be loaned to your local family history center for your use there.

The FamilySearch Wiki contains numerous helpful articles about research in Germany and links to a variety of research tools. Go to **https://familysearch.org/learn/wiki/en/Germany** to find links to these articles and to available databases and record images.

Among the many sections you'll find useful in your research are the following:

- Getting Started with German Research
- Germany Census
- Professional Genealogists Who Specialize in German Research
- German Word List
- Old German Handwriting
- Germany Gazetteers
- Germany Civil Registration

As you make progress in your research, you may want to enter your family information and photos in the Family Tree area of the Family-Search website, and also search the user-submitted genealogies to see if others have uncovered information pertinent to your family history.

The FamilySearch website is constantly being updated, and new information is always being added.

CHAPTER 4:
JEWISH RECORDS

In all my previous books I have included a separate section on Jewish records, and this book is no exception. This policy does cause me misgivings—why not separate sections on Lutherans and Catholics and Mennonites? Why not separate chapters for Saxons and Bavarians and Swabians?

However, "Jewish" is not just another religion, nor is it a distinct nationality—but the Jews are a separate people. They are separated by centuries of persecution, of subjugation, of pogroms, of the diaspora, of genocide, and finally, the concentration camps of World War II. They must be treated separately—their genealogical problems are not the same as those of other groups, their vital records are not always the same records. Their areas of research are more limited, or conversely are more widespread. Their vital events are not always recorded, or if they are, they may often be found in the records of other denominations because their own were not legally recognized.

What records will you find of Jews expelled from England in the Middle Ages—their synagogues sacked, their personal property stripped from them before they sailed? What records will there be of a child who survived a day when the Cossacks put his village to the torch and the sword? What records survive from the ghettos of a thousand Jewish settlements in Eastern Europe? What records can be found when, as recently as the middle of the last century, a Jewish family might have no family name?

Sometimes such records will exist in the most unlikely of places—be it in New York or Vienna or Tel Aviv. Yes, the problems facing Jewish ancestor-hunters are profound—but not insurmountable. There are three factors that must remain uppermost in your mind at all times: the records you need are not necessarily to be found in Jewish archives;

every year new sources of information are being discovered; and you will have problems with family names.

In the German-speaking areas of Europe, the Jewish people were subject to the same civil laws of the various states as were any other citizens, both up to the unification of Germany and since then. Civil registration started for the whole new country in 1875, but it had existed for many years before that date in several of the individual states. In many areas west of the Rhine it started in 1810, in Hannover in 1809, in Prussia in 1870, to quote just a few examples. Remember, too, that in many areas Jews could record the vital events of the family—births, marriages, and deaths—within their own community, but this had no legal basis. To protect property rights and the validity of wills, it was necessary they be recorded in the church of the state religion—be it Lutheran or Catholic. Sometimes a child's first name registered in a church differed from that recorded in a synagogue.

Probably the greatest problem facing the Jewish ancestor-hunter is that of family names, and you should give a great deal of thought and attention to this subject before you become too deeply involved in your search. Often, names were simplified or anglicized—Kanofsky became Kane, Moses became Morris, Martinez became Martin, and so on. Another complication is the literal translation of a name, so that Zevi in Hebrew became Hart in English and Hirsch in German.

Because the Jewish people, in the main, lived in isolated settlements throughout Europe from the Middle Ages onward, there was not the pressing need for a family name. "Moses, son of Aaron" was a sufficient description for recognition in a small, tightly knit community. In some cases—particularly among the Sephardim—family names based on occupations did develop in the 1600s, but they were frequently only used within the family and had no legal validity. It was not until the latter part of the eighteenth century that family names as we know them were in general use among European Jews.

In 1787 Austria ordered that all Jews should have family names; Frankfurt-am-Main followed in 1808. Napoleon enforced a similar law in the areas under his control in 1808, while Switzerland did not pass any law on the subject until 1863. When the Jewish people had to decide on a family name, their decisions were based on a wide variety of facts or fancies. Inevitably, the most popular ones were based on occupations or personal descriptions or locations—so a tailor became a Snider, a tanner a Leder (leather), a carpenter a Nagel (nail), a small man was Klein, a short one Kurtz, a religious and God-loving man was Gottlieb, a man from the east was Osterman. There were many other variations—in Frankfurt, houses were distinguished by signs instead of numbers, so very many Jews took names based on the sign on their house, and a Jew living in a house with the sign of a red shield became Rothschild, or Schiff if his house had the sign of a ship. In certain areas, such as the northwestern part of Germany, the name Rose was very popular for some unknown reason, and so in these districts there was a preponderance of names like Rose, Rosen, Rosenkrantz, Rosenbloom, Rosengarten, and so on.

Further complications are the use of patronymics (names based on that of the father)—Lewis-sohn, Aaronson, Abrahamson, Myerson—and on matronymics (names based on that of the mother)—Perle, Perlson, Gutkind, and so on. Patronymics and matronymics were used, too, in a more general way—in Slavic areas Wicz or Vitch were added to the father's or mother's first name; in Romania it would be Vici, in German areas Sohn or Witz.

For the above reasons it is often difficult to trace your Jewish ancestry back beyond the 1700s unless you have some family documentation to guide you. You may even find that after your ancestors had a recognized family name, they changed it to that of a revered rabbi or a well-known Talmudic scholar.

For a list of online databases and websites pertaining to German Jewish genealogy, go to the website of the German Jewish Special Interest Group (GerSIG) at **www.jewishgen.org/gersig/**. In addition, several years ago Landesarchiv Baden-Wuerttemberg (**www.landesarchiv-bw.de/web/**) put images online of civil registration books from 1810 to 1870, as well as family books and other records primarily from the nineteenth century.

The Family History Library has over 2,000 microfilms of German Jewish birth, marriage, and death records; other Jewish records at the Family History Library include synagogue records, records of Jewish taxpayers, Holocaust victims, and censuses. Check out the Jewish Genealogy Research page at **https://familysearch.org/learn/wiki/en/Jewish_Genealogy_Research** for more information about the holdings of the Family History Library and a rundown of Jewish records available on the Internet.

Some useful addresses in Germany are:

Museum jüdischer Geschichte und Kultur (Museum of Jewish History
    and Culture)
Treibgasse 20
63739 Aschaffenburg
Phone: 011-49-60-21-29-087
E-mail: museum@aschaffenburg.de
Website: www.museen-aschaffenburg.de/

Jüdisches Kulturmuseum (Jewish Culture Museum)
Halderstrasse 8
86150 Augsburg
Phone: 011-49-8-21-513-658
E-mail: office@jkmas.de
Website: www.jkmas.de/

Jüdisches Museum Berlin
Lindenstrasse 9-14
10969 Berlin
Phone: 011-49-30-25-993-300
E-mail: info@jmberlin.de
Website: www.jmberlin.de

Jüdisches Museum Westfalen
Julius-Ambrunn-Strasse 1
46282 Dorsten
Phone: 011-49-2-36-245-279
E-mail: info@jmw-dorsten.de
Website: www.jmw-dorsten.de/

Archiv, Stiftung Neue Synagoge Berlin—Centrum Judaicum
Oranienburger Strasse 28-30
10117 Berlin
Phone: 011-49-30-88-028-425
E-mail: archiv@centrumjudaicum.de
Website: www.centrumjudaicum.de/cj-archiv/

Zentralarchiv zur Erforschung der Geschichte der Juden in
 Deutschland
Landfriedstrasse 12
69117 Heidelberg
Phone: 011-49-6-22-116-4141
E-mail: zentralarchiv@uni-hd.de
Website: www.zentralarchiv.uni-hd.de

So far as Jewish records in Europe are concerned, be sure you do
not overlook the Hamburg Passenger Lists because this port and that of
Bremen were the main places from which the emigrants from north and
central Europe sailed to the New World (see Chapter 6 for full details
about these passenger records).

If you already know the place from which your ancestors came, be
sure you contact the local public library because many of the larger
centers have Jewish collections containing a great deal of information
about families in the area. These include detailed histories of Jewish
communities. You will find that archivists and librarians are very helpful
to Jewish inquirers from overseas.

The Weissensee Cemetery (Herbert-Baum-Strasse 45, 13088 Berlin; website: www.jg-berlin.org/en/judaism/cemeteries/weissensee.html) is the largest Jewish cemetery in Europe. In the offices are over 115,000 index cards that give full details of each person buried there for over a century. You can also obtain details from Zentralarchiv zur Erforschung der Geschichte der Juden in Deutschland (Landfriedstrasse 12, 69117 Heidelberg; e-mail: Zentralarchiv@urz.uni-heidelberg.de; website: www.uni-heidelberg.de/institute/sonst/aj/).

The Jewish Cemetery Altona (Königstrasse 10a, 22767 Hamburg; website: www.jüdischer-friedhof-altona.de/english.html), dating back to 1611, is the oldest Jewish cemetery in Hamburg and the oldest Portuguese-Sephardic Jewish cemetery in northern Europe. There are more than 6,000 German and 1,600 Portuguese gravestones, which are completely or fragmentarily preserved. You can see some photos of the cemetery at **www.txmx.de/grafix/jufried**. A list of Jewish cemeteries in Germany is available online at **www.uni-heidelberg.de/institute/sonst/aj/FRIEDHOF/ALLGEM/index.html**. The Hamburg Staatsarchiv has a register of the Jewish community in that city dating back to 1769.

In the Middle Ages the cities of Speyer, Worms, and Mainz were home to illustrious Jewish communities. Worms still has the most evidence of Jewish life in the past, including the oldest surviving Jewish cemetery in Europe.

The International Tracing Service archive (ITS), located in Bad Arolsen, Germany, documents the fate of the victims of Nazi persecution. Its archives contain about 30 million documents on concentration camps, Gestapo prisons, and ghettos, as well as on forced labor and displaced persons. The alphabetically and phonetically arranged Central Name Index contains over 50 million reference cards for over 17.5 million people.

The ITS is in the process of digitizing all of its records. You can consult ITS documents at Yad Vashem in Jerusalem; the U.S. Holocaust Memorial Museum in Washington, D.C.; the Institute for National Remembrance in Warsaw; the Centre for Documentation and Research on Resistance in Luxembourg; the Belgian State Archives in Brussels; the French National Archives in Paris; and the Wiener Library in London. For more information about the ITS, consult its website, **www.its-arolsen.org/english/index.html**.

The Central Database of Shoah Victims' Names is an international undertaking initiated and led by Yad Vashem, with the goal of recovering the names and reconstructing the life stories of each Jew murdered in the Holocaust. By the beginning of 2014, about 4.3 million Jews had been added to the database, which is searchable at **http://db.yadvashem.org/names/search.html?language=en**.

Outside of Germany proper you will find Jewish records in other archives, in what we call the Germanic area so far as language is concerned:

Austria

Jewish records are quite prolific for this country and are to be found in state archives, municipal offices, and magistrate's courts. Most of the record books of Jewish births, marriages, and deaths in Vienna from the early 1800s to 1938 have survived and are located at the headquarters of the Vienna Jewish Community; for more information contact Israelitische Kultusgemeinde Wien (Seitenstettengasse 4, 1010 Vienna; e-mail: office@ikg-wien.at; website: www.ikg-wien.at/).

Access to the Austrian Jewish cemetery databases is available over the Internet. The IKG database has 153,622 entries for people deceased prior to May 5, 1945, and is accessible at **http://friedhof.ikg-wien.at/search. asp?lang=en**. The Documentation Centre of Austrian Resistance, **www. doew.at**, has a large archive and library with a lot of information on the Holocaust, including an Oral History collection with more than 1,000 interviews, and a searchable database containing over 63,000 Austrian Holocaust victims. A database of Austrian victims is also searchable at **www.lettertothestars.at/en/liste_opfer.php**.

When the Germans occupied Vienna in 1938, all Jewish residents had to complete a detailed declaration of their property, including bank accounts, insurance policies, real estate, art, etc. These declarations are in the files of the State Archives in Vienna.

Hungary

There are a number of microfilms available of Jewish communities in the German-speaking areas of Hungary, and these are located in the National Archives of Hungary (Magyar Orzágos Levéltár, Bécsi kapu tér 4, 1014 Budapest; phone: 011-36-1-225-2843; e-mail: info@mol. gov.hu; website: www.mol.gov.hu/). Yad Vashem (see below) has a computerized list of half a million Hungarian victims of the Holocaust.

The JewishGen Hungary Database, **www.jewishgen.org/databases/ Hungary/**, searches fourteen databases with information on Hungarian Jews, including one with 300,000 names of Hungarian Holocaust victims and survivors.

Poland

Jewish Records Indexing (JRI-Poland), **http://jri-poland.org/jriintro. htm,** is the largest fully searchable database of indexes to Jewish vital records accessible online. Five million records from more than 550 Polish towns are now indexed, with more being added every few months.

The Eastern European Archival Database, **www.rtrfoundation.org/ search.php**, includes documents from civil registration offices in Poland and the Jewish Historical Institute in Warsaw, Poland.

Some of the various regional archives have Jewish records from what were German-speaking areas, such as Bytom (Beuthen), Kraków, Gdańsk (Danzig), Legnica (Liegnitz), Opole (Oppeln), Posnań (Posen), Warszawa (Warsaw), Wrocław (Breslau), and Zielona Góra (Grünberg). Many of these have been microfilmed by the Central Archives for the History of the Jewish People in Jerusalem. Yad Vashem has a computerized list of 204,000 residents of the Łódź ghetto, with dates of birth, death, and deportation. (See below for addresses for the Central Archives and Yad Vashem.) The Łódź KehilaLinks website, **http://kehilalinks. jewishgen.org/lodz/index.htm**, contains original articles and hundreds of links to documents, interviews, and photographs on Łódź and surrounding communities.

ISRAEL

There are a variety of sources in Israel:

The National Library of Israel
The Hebrew University of Jerusalem
Edmond J. Safra Campus, Givat Ram
POB 39105 Jerusalem, Israel
Phone: 011-74-733-6336
Website: http://jnul.huji.ac.il/

Central Archives for the History of the Jewish People
The Hebrew University of Jerusalem
The Edmond J. Safra Campus, Givat Ram
POB 39077, Jerusalem 91390
Tel. 011-972-2-658-6249
E-mail: cahjp@nli.org.il
Website: http://sites.huji.ac.il/archives

Douglas E. Goldman Jewish Genealogy Center
Beit Hatfutsot/The Museum of the Jewish People
P.O. Box 39359, Tel Aviv 6139202
Phone: 011-972-3-745-7808
E-mail: tours@bh.org.il
Website: www.bh.org.il/databases/jewish-genealogy/

Ghetto Fighters' House Museum
D. N. Western Galilee, 25220

Phone: 011-972-4-995-8080
Website: www.gfh.org.il/

Yad Vashem
The Holocaust Martyrs' and Heroes' Remembrance Authority
P.O. Box 3477, Jerusalem 9103401
Phone: 011-972-2-644-3720
E-mail: general.information@yadvashem.org.il
Website: www.yadvashem.org/

THE UNITED STATES

In the United States, you will find almost all of the records you need for your German Jewish research.

Center for Jewish History
15 West 16th Street
New York, NY 10011
Phone: 212-294-8301. Fax: 212-294-8302
E-mail: inquiries@cjh.org
Website: www.cjh.org

The most dramatic development in Jewish record-keeping in North America in recent years has been the creation of the Center for Jewish History. Five organizations have joined together to establish a world center for research into Jewish history—including, of course, Jewish genealogical research. The five organizations' archival collections span more than 700 years of history and total over 500,000 volumes and 100 million documents. The collections, which are searchable online, also include thousands of artworks, textiles, ritual objects, recordings, films, and photographs.

The building encompasses 125,000 square feet of space in this five-section, multi-level complex. The computer system provides worldwide access to the treasures that are being accumulated from Israel, archival treasures of the member organizations, and individual collections.

The organizations housed in the Center for Jewish History facility are given below, with contact information:

- **American Jewish Historical Society;** phone: 212-294-6160; fax: 212-294-6161; e-mail: info@ajhs.cjh.org; website: www.ajhs.org/
- **American Sephardi Federation;** phone: 212-294-8350; fax: 212-294-8348; e-mail: info@sephardi.house; website: www.sephardi.house
- **Leo Baeck Institute;** phone: 212-744-6400; fax: 212-988-1305; e-mail: lbaeck@lbi.cjh.org; website: www.lbi.org/

- **Yeshiva University Museum (YUM);** phone: 212-294-8330; fax: 212-294-8335; e-mail: info@yum.cjh.org; website: www. yumuseum.org/
- **YIVO Institute for Jewish Research;** phone: 212-246-6080; fax: 212-292-1892; e-mail: yivoinquiries@cjh.org; website: www.yivo. org/

   (The Leo Baeck Institute specializes in the German-speaking areas of Europe; the YIVO Institute specializes in East European Jewry.)

The New York Public Library (Dorot Jewish Division)
Fifth Avenue at 42nd Street
New York, NY 10018
Phone: 212-930-0601. Fax: 212-642-0141
E-mail: freidus@nypl.org
Website: www.nypl.org/locations/schwarzman/jewish-division

This has one of the largest collections of Judaica in the world, and the second largest collection of yizkor books in the city (second only to the YIVO Institute). It is impossible to list all the holdings, but the German collections include tombstone inscriptions from Köln, Nürnberg, Speyer, and Worms; genealogies from Germany and Lithuania; and records of many Jewish communities from the Germanic areas of Europe. You could happily and profitably spend two or three days here. The majority of their yizkor books are available online at **http://legacy. www.nypl.org/research/chss/jws/yizkorbookonline.cfm**.

There are two other organizations in the city that may also be of value to you:

The Jewish Theological Seminary Library
3080 Broadway
New York, NY 10027
Phone: 212-678-8082. Fax: 212-678-8891
E-mail: library@jtsa.edu
Website: www.jtsa.edu/Library.xml

The Mendel Gottesman Library of Hebraica and Judaica
Yeshiva University, 2520 Amsterdam Avenue
New York, NY 10033
Phone: 212-960-5382
Website: www.yu.edu/libraries/about/mendel-gottesman-library/

Outside New York City there are the following organizations:

American Jewish Archives
3101 Clifton Avenue
Cincinnati, OH 45220

Phone: 513-221-1875. Fax: 513-221-7812
Website: www.americanjewisharchives.org/

American Jewish Historical Society, New England Archives
99-101 Newbury Street
Boston, MA 02116-3062
Phone: 617-226-1245. Fax: 617-226-1248
E-mail: reference@ajhsboston.org
Website: http://ajhsboston.org/

The National Archives at College Park
8601 Adelphi Road
College Park, MD 20740
Phone: 301-837-2000
Website: www.archives.gov/dc-metro/college-park/

The National Archives holds over 70,000 rolls of microfilm of cap-
tured German records and related documents, including registers of
German concentration camp inmates and index cards filmed at the Berlin
Document Center listing the name, date and place of birth, occupation,
and last address of Jews whose German citizenship was revoked in ac-
cordance with the Nürnberg Laws of 1935.

CANADA

The Canadian Jewish Congress Charities Committee (CJCCC) National
    Archives
1590 Docteur Penfield Avenue
Montreal, Quebec, H3G 1C5
Phone: 514-931-7531
E-mail: archives@cjccc.ca
Website: www.cjccc.ca/national_archives

The CJCCC archives collects and preserves documentation on all
aspects of the Jewish presence in Quebec and Canada.

Jewish Genealogical Society of Canada (Toronto)
P.O. Box 91006
2901 Bayview Avenue
Toronto ON M2K 2Y6
Phone: 647-247-6414
E-mail: info@jgstoronto.ca
Website: www.jgstoronto.ca/

A Guide to Canadian Jewish Genealogical Research can be found at **www.jewishgen.org/InfoFiles/Canada/index.html**.

Finally, do not be discouraged by your Jewish ancestral difficulties—bring to the search the tenacity, the patience, the determination, the intelligence, and the deep attachment to history of your ancestors.

CHAPTER 5:
CHURCH RECORDS

Some church records date back to the fifteenth century, but in fact you should not expect to find many of them before about 1563 for the Catholic Church—when the Council of Trent first mandated the recording of vital records by churches—and a few years later for the Lutherans. Some of the exceptions are to be found in Baden and Württemberg, where there are Lutheran and Catholic registers dating back to the early 1500s.

Although civil registration did not come into force until recent times, very early church registers often contained detailed information about individuals in the parish. Remember, of course, that most church records showed only dates of baptism, marriage, and burial, and you may never find out the dates of birth and death.

Many of the registers have been destroyed as the result of civil wars, rebellions, and invasions over the centuries, but in some cases duplicates were kept in a separate location, so all is not necessarily lost. In Mecklenburg, for example, copies were kept from 1740 onward.

If you are searching church registers in person, you must be prepared to cope with entries in Latin (until the mid-nineteenth century) and the old German script, plus bad handwriting, and even a style of handwriting that is very different from that of the present day. No one ever said ancestor-hunting was easy!

Illegitimacy was fairly common in some rural areas of Germany. The illegitimate children were always baptized, but often the entry was made upside-down or sideways to emphasize the difference. The entry itself was very specific. The child was a bastard (Hurenkind), the mother a whore (Hure), and the father a fornicator (Hurer) or an adulterer (Ehebrecher).

The entries in the church registers usually include the following information:

BAPTISMS: Name, sex, date, names of parents, father's occupation, place of birth, names and addresses of godparents.

MARRIAGES: Name, age, and address of bride and bridegroom, occupation of groom, names and addresses of parents, occupation of the two fathers.

BURIALS: Name, age, place of death, cause of death, names of parents, name of husband or wife if still alive, date and place of burial.

Usually the above entries were made in three separate registers, but occasionally you will find all three events entered in one register in chronological order as they occurred.

In some parishes, particularly in the eighteenth and nineteenth centuries, you may find Family Books (Familienbücher or Liber de Statu Animarum). These contained complete records of a family and are of great genealogical value. Always check in a particular locality with the Catholic priest or the Lutheran minister as to the existence of a Family Book. The book showed the name of the head of the household at the time the entry was made, the full names of the various members of the household, their places of birth, their marital status, the dates of death of deceased family members, and the place to which a family member moved if he or she left home (for marriage, work, or emigration).

Check also for Kirchenbuchduplikate, a duplicate of entries in the church register, which was sent each year to the nearest headquarters of the particular church.

Sometimes you will find the vital records of dissidents such as Amish, Brethren, Jews, and Mennonites recorded in the church book of the then-ruler's denomination, or in a separate section of the book. Other times those records were moved to one of the few tolerant places of refuge, such as Neuwied on the Rhine.

A major new development to help facilitate access to German church records is the Kirchenbuchportal (church book portal) Internet site. As of this writing, about 35,000 individual church books in Germany (approximately 25 percent of the total) have been digitized. Most of the German Protestant regional church bodies are participating in this project; Catholic and other denomination archives and civil registrations may join in later. There will be a fee to use this service. Go to **www. kirchenbuchportal.de/** for more information.

Matricula (**http://matricula-online.eu**) is an online repository of scanned images of church records from Austria and Germany, including both Roman Catholic and Lutheran records. Among the German church records in this collection are Lutheran Church records from the Rhineland, Pfalz, and the central archives in Berlin and Pfalz, and Roman Catholic records from Passau.

Pre-1900 Alsatian church records have been digitized and are available online at **http://etat-civil.bas-rhin.fr/adeloch/index.php** and **http:// www.archives.cg68.fr/**.

Numerous German church records have been microfilmed by the LDS Family History Library; check the FamilySearch website at **https:// familysearch.org** to see what is available. Keep in mind that the FamilySearch catalog organizes records according to the political divisions of the German Empire of 1871, not today's jurisdictions.

THE EVANGELICAL CHURCH

The Evangelical Church in Germany (Evangelische Kirche in Deutschland—abbreviated as EKD) is a union of twenty-three Lutheran, Reformed, and United regional churches:

Evangelische Kirche in Deutschland (EKD)
Herrenhäuser Strasse 12
30419 Hanover
Phone: 011-49-511-2796-0. Fax: 011-49-511-2796-707
E-mail: info@ekd.de
Website: www.ekd.de/

Below are the addresses, phone and fax numbers, and URLs for the various EKD churches.

Evangelische Landeskirche Anhalts
Friedrichstrasse 22, 06844 Dessau-Rosslau
Phone: 011-49-340-2526-0. Fax: 011-49-340-2526-130
Website: www.landeskirche-anhalts.de/

Evangelische Landeskirche in Baden
Blumenstrasse 1-7, 76133 Karlsruhe
Phone: 011-49-721-9175-0. Fax: 011-49-721-9175-550
Website: www.ekiba.de/

Evangelisch-Lutherische Kirche in Bayern (Bavaria)
Katharina von Bora 11-13, 80333 Munich (München)
Phone: 011-49-89-5595-0. Fax: 011-49-89-5595-666
Website: www.bayern-evangelisch.de/

Evangelische Kirche in Berlin-Brandenburg-schlesische Oberlausitz
Georgenkirchstrasse 69, 10249 Berlin
Phone: 011-49-30-24344-121. Fax: 011-49-30-24344-500
Website: www.ekbo.de/

Evangelisch-Lutherische Landeskirche in Braunschweig (Brunswick)
Dietrich-Bonhoeffer-Strasse 1, 38300 Wolfenbüttel
Phone: 011-49-533-1802-0. Fax: 011-49-533-1802-707
Website: www.landeskirche-braunschweig.de/

Bremische Evangelische Kirche
Franziuseck 2-4, 28199 Bremen

Phone: 011-49-421-5597-0. Fax: 011-49-421-5597-265
Website: www.kirche-bremen.de/

Evangelisch-Lutherische Landeskirche Hannovers (Hanover)
Rote Reihe 6, 30169 Hannover
Phone: 011-49-511-1241-0. Fax: 011-49-511-1241-266
Website: www.evlka.de/

Evangelische Kirche in Hessen und Nassau (Hesse and Nassau)
Paulusplatz 1, 64285 Darmstadt
Phone: 011-49-61-51405-0. Fax: 011-49-61-51405-220
Website: www.ekhn.de/

Evangelische Kirche von Kurhessen-Waldeck
Wilhelmshöher Allee 330, 34131 Kassel
Phone: 011-49-561-9378-0. Fax: 011-49-561-9378-400
Website: www.ekkw.de/

Lippische Landeskirche
Leopoldstrasse 27, 32756 Detmold
Phone: 011-49-5231-9766-0. Fax: 011-49-5231-9768-50
Website: www.lippische-landeskirche.de/

Evangelisch-Lutherischer Kirchenkreis Mecklenburg
Münzstrasse 8-10, 19055 Schwerin
Phone: 011-49-385-20223-147-147. Fax: 011-49-385-20223-162
Website: www.kirche-mv.de/

Landeskirchenamt der Evangelischen Kirche in Mitteldeutschland
Michaelisstrasse 39, 99084 Erfurt
Phone: 011-49-361-51800-0. Fax: 011-49-361-51800-198
Website: www.ekmd.de/

Evangelisch-Lutherische Kirche in Norddeutschland
Königsstrasse 54, 22767 Hamburg
Phone: 011-49-40-306-20-1100
Website: www.nordkirche.de/

Evangelisch-Lutherische Kirche in Oldenburg
Philosophenweg 1, 26121 Oldenburg
Phone: 011-49-441-7701-0. Fax: 011-49-441-7701-2199
Website: www.kirche-oldenburg.de/

Evangelische Kirche der Pfalz (Protestantische Landeskirche)
Domplatz 5, 67346 Speyer
Phone: 011-49-62-32-6670. Fax: 011-49-62-32-667-480
Website: www.evkirchepfalz.de/

Pommerscher Evangelischer Kirchenkreis (Pomerania)
Bahnhofstrasse 35/36, 17489 Greifswald
Phone: 011-49-3834-554-6. Fax: 011-49-3834-554-799
Website: www.kirche-mv.de

Evangelisch-reformierten Kirche
Grosse Kirche
Reformierter Kirchgang 17, 26789 Leer
Phone: 011-49-491-2566
Website: www.reformiert.de/

Evangelische Kirche im Rheinland (Rhineland)
Hans-Böckler Strasse 7, 40476 Düsseldorf
Phone: 011-49-211-45-62-0. Fax: 011-49-211-45-62-444
Website: www.ekir.de/

Evangelisch-Lutherische Landeskirche Sachsens
Lukasstrasse 6, 01069 Dresden
Phone: 011-49-351-4692-0. Fax: 011-49-351-4692-109
Website: www.evlks.de/

Evangelisch-Lutherische Kirchengemeinde Sachsenhagen
Holztrift 1, 31553 Sachsenhagen
Phone: 011-49-5725-9150-00
Website: www.kirche-sachsenhagen.de/

Evangelische Kirche von Westfalen (Westphalia)
Altstädter Kirchplatz 5, 33602 Bielefeld
Phone: 011-49-521-594-0. Fax: 011-49-521-594-129
Website: www.evangelisch-in-westfalen.de/

Evangelische Landeskirche in Württemberg
Augustenstrasse 124, 70197 Stuttgart
Phone: 011-49-711-222-76-58. Fax: 011-49-711-222-76-81
Website: www.elk-wue.de/

As you can see, in the past the Protestant churches in Germany were divided into several sects. If you know your emigrant ancestor from Germany was a member of the Evangelical Church, it will help you in your search if you can discover just which sect he belonged to in the old country.

You will find the staff of the various church headquarters to be very helpful, but you must not ask for the impossible. For example, people have been known to write to the North Elbian Evangelical Lutheran Church to the effect "My great-grandfather was a member of the Evangelical Church and came from somewhere near you. He was born in 1870 or thereabouts. Can you look up the baptism entry in the register?" The North Elbian area covers Schleswig-Holstein, Hamburg, Eutin, and Lübeck. You can imagine how impossible it would be to even start to search. The websites listed above usually contain contact forms and/or e-mail addresses to use for your queries. If you can, write in German. If you cannot, then at least end your letter with the words "Mit freundlichen Grüssen" ("With friendly greetings").

Churches in East Prussia (Ostpreussen)

Before the invasion of East Prussia by the Red Army, the parish registers and church books (Kirchenbücher) from about 500 parishes were removed to what was then West Berlin. They are in the Evangelical Central Archives in Berlin (Evangelisches Zentralarchiv in Berlin, Bethaniendamm 29, 10997 Berlin; website: www.ezab.de/).

The Evangelical Central Archives collects personal papers of important evangelical personages, documents of associations, and societies of cross-regional importance. Its holdings include about 6,000 parish registers from German parishes belonging to the former Prussian church.

The Family History Library has a collection of microfilmed Lutheran records from Memel and the Memel area covering the period 1614–1944. Several archives, including the archives in Russia for this region, may have received the originals after the filming. Some church books from Memel are in the Lithuanian Central State Archives in Vilnius.

The Lutheran Church in North America

Since your German ancestors may have been members of the church in both the Germanic area of Europe and later in North America, you should be aware of changes that took place in 1986 in the organization of the church in both the United States and Canada. The various mergers that took place may change the locations of the church headquarters in both countries. This may also have an effect on the location of the church archives.

In the United States three Lutheran churches agreed to merge into a single church—the Evangelical Lutheran Church in America (ELCA), with national headquarters in Chicago. The three churches concerned were the Lutheran Church in America, the American Lutheran Church, and the Association of Evangelical Lutheran Churches. The Lutheran Church-Missouri Synod remained separate because it is more conservative and does not practice open communion or allow women to be ordained as ministers. They are also more literal in their interpretation of the scriptures.

In Canada the three districts of the Lutheran Church in America acted jointly through the Lutheran Church in America—Canada Section. The Canadian counterpart of the American Lutheran Church has been independent since 1971 and was known as the Evangelical Lutheran Church of Canada (ELCC). The ELCC and the three synods of the Lutheran Church in America merged on January 1, 1986 and are now called the Evangelical Lutheran Church in Canada (ELCIC). The church headquarters are located at 600-177 Lombard Avenue, Winnipeg, MB R3B 0W5 (website: www.elcic.ca). There are a few other Lutheran groups in Canada, which total about one percent of the Lutheran population.

The Lutheran Church—Canada was founded in 1988 when the Canadian congregations of the Lutheran Church—Missouri Synod formed an autonomous Canadian church with three districts, one in Edmonton, Alberta; one in Regina, Saskatchewan; and one in East District in Kitchener, Ontario.

THE CATHOLIC CHURCH

The Catholic Church in Germany is organized in ecclesiastical provinces (each under an archbishop), bishoprics (Bistum), and the local parish (Pfarr). There are twenty-seven church archives. These hold the earlier parish registers, as well as confirmation and communion records, and in many cases, the Family Books (Liber de Statu Animarum). There is no countrywide accepted date for the surrender of early records to the various archives.

The Family Books were first introduced in 1614 and include full details of each family in the parish, together with the names of any servants and the occupation of the head of the family. The books were kept in Latin and German and are more complete in some areas than in others. It was compulsory for the priest to maintain the books up to 1918, but since then it has been quite voluntary. The division of Germany after World War II did not affect the boundaries of the various dioceses, and so the re-unification in 1990 had no effect on ecclesiastical divisions.

The address of the Catholic Church headquarters is as follows:

Sekretariat der Deutschen Bischofskonferenz
Kaiserstrasse 161, 53113 Bonn
Phone: 011-49-228-103-214. Fax: 011-49-228-103-254
Website: http://dbk.de/

The addresses of the various Catholic Archives are set out below. You can also find a listing of them at **www.katholisch.de/**. It should not be difficult for you to decide to which address you should write. If, for example, your ancestors came from Wanzleben, a gazetteer or a good map in your local library will show you it is near Magdeburg, and the list below will give you the address for that diocese. Generally speaking, you will find that the headquarters of each Bistum are located in the largest city of the area:

Klosterplatz 7, 52062 **Aachen**
Phone: 011-49-241-452-0. Fax: 011-49-241-452-436
Website: www.kirche-im-bistum-aachen.de/

Fronhof 4, 86152 **Augsburg**
Phone: 011-49-821-3166-0. Fax: 011-49-821-3166-419
Website: www.bistum-augsburg.de/

Domplatz 2, 96049 **Bamberg**
Phone: 011-49-951-502-1500. Fax: 011-49-951-502-1509
Website: http://erzbistum.kirche-bamberg.de/

Niederwallstrasse 8-9, 10117 **Berlin**
Phone: 011-49-30-3268-40. Fax: 011-49-30-3268-4193
Website: www.erzbistumberlin.de/

Käthe-Kollwitz-Ufer 84, 01309 **Dresden**
Phone: 011-49-351-3364-600. Fax: 011-49-351-3364-791
Website: www.bistum-dresden-meissen.de/

Luitpoldstrasse 2, 85072 **Eichstätt**
Phone: 011-49-8421-50-0. Fax: 011-49-8421-50-259
Website: www.bistum-eichstaett.de/

Hermannsplatz 9, 99084 **Erfurt**
Phone: 011-49-361-6572-0. Fax: 011-49-361-6572-444
Website: www.bistum-erfurt.de/

Zwölfling 16, 45127 **Essen**
Phone: 011-49-201-2204-1. Fax: 011-49-201-2204-570
Website: www.bistum-essen.de/

Schoferstrasse 2, 79098 **Freiburg**
Phone: 011-49-761-2188-0. Fax: 011-49-761-2188-505
Website: www.erzbistum-freiburg.de/

Paulustor 5, 36037 **Fulda**
Phone: 011-49-661-87-0. Fax: 011-49-661-87-578
Website: www.bistum-fulda.de/

Carl-von-Ossietzky-Strasse 41, 02826 **Görlitz**
Phone: 011-49-3581-4782-0. Fax: 011-49-3581-4782-12
Website: www.bistum-goerlitz.de/

Am Mariendom 4, 20099 **Hamburg**
Phone: 011-49-40-248-77-100. Fax: 011-49-40-248-77-233
Website: www.erzbistum-hamburg.de/

Domhof 18-21, 31134 **Hildesheim**
Phone: 011-49-5121-307-0. Fax: 011-49-5121-307-488
Website: www.bistum-hildesheim.de/

Marzellenstrasse 32, 50668 **Köln**
Phone: 011-49-221-1642-0. Fax: 011-49-221-1642-1700
Website: www.erzbistum-koeln.de/

Rossmarkt 4, 65549 **Limburg**
Phone: 011-49-643-1295-0. Fax: 011-49-643-1295-476
Website: www.bistumlimburg.de/

Max-Josef-Metzger-Strasse 1, 39104 **Magdeburg**
Phone: 011-49-391-5961-0. Fax: 011-49-391-5961-100
Website: www.bistum-magdeburg.de/

Bischofsplatz 2, 55116 **Mainz**
Phone: 011-49-6131-253-100. Fax: 011-49-6131-253-585
Website: www.bistummainz.de/

Postfach 33 03 60, 80063 **München**
Phone: 011-49-89-2137-0. Fax: 011-49-89-2137-1585
Website: www.erzbistum-muenchen.de/

Domplatz 27, 48143 **Münster**
Phone: 011-49-251-495-0. Fax: 011-49-251-495-6086
Website: www.bistummuenster.de/

Hasestrasse 40a, 49074 **Osnabrück**
Phone: 011-49-541-318-0. Fax: 011-49-541-318-117
Website: www.bistum-osnabrueck.de/

Domplatz 3, 33098 **Paderborn**
Phone: 011-49-525-1125-1287. Fax: 011-49-525-1125-470
Website: www.erzbistum-paderborn.de/

Residenzplatz 8, 94032 **Passau**
Phone: 011-49-851-393-0. Fax: 011-49-851-393-830
Website: www.bistum-passau.de/

Niedermünstergasse 1, 93047 **Regensburg***
Phone: 011-49-941-597-01. Fax: 011-49-941-597-1055
Website: www.bistum-regensburg.de/

Eugen-Bolz-Platz 1, 72108 **Rottenburg**
Phone: 011-49-7472-169-0. Fax: 011-49-7472-169-561
Website: www.drs.de/

Kleine Pfaffengasse 16, 67346 **Speyer**
Phone: 011-49-6232-102-0. Fax: 011-49-6232-102-300
Website: http://cms.bistum-speyer.de/www2/

Hinter dem Dom 6, 54290 **Trier** (Postfach 1340, 54203 Trier)
Phone: 011-49-651-7105-0. Fax: 011-49-651-7105-498
Website: http://cms.bistum-trier.de/

---

*A number of church registers from West Prussia are now in these archives. If your Catholic ancestors came from a known location in West Prussia you should check whether the registers are here.

Domerschulstrasse 2, 97070 **Würzburg**
Phone: 011-49-931-386-0. Fax: 011-49-931-386-334
Website: www.bistum-wuerzburg.de/

The church registers are either in the original parish church or in one of the church archives listed above. Unfortunately, there is no hard-and-fast rule that says that registers must be sent to the archives on a certain date. In fact, there is no law at all controlling this matter. Even if a church is closed, it is not possible to say with certainty that the registers were then lodged in the church archives. They may have been transferred to the nearest church remaining in operation.

If you know the exact location of the place from which your ancestor came, you can probably identify the particular archive that may have the registers. If you cannot, then I would write to the Sekretariat and ask where the registers for that particular church are now.

PARISH ARCHIVES

Given below are separate church archives known to exist and *not* included in the major church archives listed above. After the province code, a C or L is given in parentheses to indicate whether the archives hold Catholic or Lutheran records, or both.

Amöneburg (H) (C)
Balingen (BW) (L)
Biberach (BW) (L and C)
Bochum (NW) (L)
Bottrop (NW) (C)
Brakel (NW) (C)
Burgsteinfurt (NW) (L and C)
Duderstadt (NS) (L and C)
Duisburg (NW) (L)
Dulmen (NW) (L)
Emden (NS) (L)
Emmerich (NW) (L and C)
Engelskirchen (NW) (C)
Erfurt (T) (L and C)
Essen (H) (C)
Flensburg (SH) (C)
Göttingen (NS) (L and C)
Gudow (SH) (L)
Hagen (NW) (L and C)

Hattingen (NW) (L)
Herford (NW) (L and C)
Herrenberg (BW) (L)
Hof (B) (L)
Höxter (NW) (C)
Isny (BW) (L)
Karlsruhe (BW) (L)
Kassel (H) (L)
Kulmbach (B) (C)
Leer (H) (L)
Lich (H) (L)
Lübeck (SH) (L)
Methler (NW) (L)
Molzen (NS) (L)
Munstereifel (NW) (L)
Neuss (NW) (L)
Remagen (RP) (L and C)
Rottweil (BW) (C)
St. Goar (RP) (L)

Schwäbisch Hall (BW) (L)
Siegburg (NW) (C)
Stockum (NW) (C)
Überlingen (BW) (C)
Uelzen (NS) (L)

Viersen (NW) (C)
Wattenscheid (NW) (L and C)
Wetzlar (H) (L and C)
Xanten (NW) (C)
Zweibrücken (RP) (L)

OTHER RELIGIOUS GROUPS

The two largest of the Protestant free churches, the Methodists and the Evangelical Community (Evangelische-Gemeinschaft), joined in 1968 to form the Evangelical Methodist Church (Evangelisch-Methodistische Kirche; website: www.emk.de/). There is also the Alliance of Free Evangelical Congregations (website: www.ead.de/)—Baptists (Bund Evangelisch-Freikirchlicher—Baptisten), as well as Mennonites, Quakers, and Jews (see Chapter 4 for more information about Jewish records). By and large, all these organizations leave the registers and other records in the individual churches.

THE CALENDAR

Before searching German records, you should be aware of changes in the calendar that, over a period of some years, produced either opposing and contradictory systems, or two different systems existing side by side.

Until 1582 the Julian calendar, established by Julius Caesar, was used in Germany and, indeed, in all civilized countries. This calendar divided the year into 365 days, plus an extra day every fourth year. The system was in operation until 1582, but astronomers had discovered that it exceeded the solar year by eleven minutes—or three days every four hundred years. Between the date when the Julian calendar was established in 325 and the year 1582, the difference amounted to eleven days. Since this affected the calculations for Easter, Pope Gregory XIII decreed that ten days be dropped from the calendar in order to bring Easter to the correct date. To prevent a recurrence of the problem, he also ordered that in every four hundred years leap year's extra day be omitted in a centennial year when the first two digits could not be divided by four without a remainder.

Are you still with me? Well, it means that it was omitted in 1700, 1800, and 1900 but was not omitted in 2000. The Pope also changed the beginning of the New Year from March 25 to January 1, and this new system became known as the Gregorian calendar.

Generally speaking, the new calendar came into force in Germany between 1582 and 1585, depending on the locality. There were some places that started it later and the most important of these are listed below:

Prussia (Preussen)	1612
Pfalz-Neuburg	1615
Osnabrück	1624
Minden	1630
Hildesheim	1631
Friesland	1700

Basically, the Protestant areas were reluctant to make the change, while the Catholic areas started as soon as possible after the papal decree was issued. So you will find places where the Catholic Church accepted the New Year as starting on January 1 and so called September the ninth month, while the Lutheran Church in the same place regarded March 25 as the New Year and regarded September as the seventh month.

When the change did take place, it led to confusing entries of dates in church registers for a brief period. Once the reason is clear to you, you will not be puzzled to find that an ancestress of yours had one child born in one year and a second born a few months later. It was the calendar that changed and not the nine-month gestation period, so all is well!

OTHER CHURCH RECORDS

Grave Registers (Grabregister)

These were maintained in the parish church, and although they were a duplicate of the entry of burial in the church register, they often contained additional information such as the date of death and the exact age (i.e., 38 years, 204 days). As the burial entries usually gave the date of *burial* and the age only in years, the grave registers can be of great help.

Church Receipt Books (Einnahmebücher)

These gave details of payments received from church members for such services as bell-tolling for a funeral (with name of deceased and date), and payment for burial plots and funeral cloths (Leichenhemden).

Confirmation Records (Konfirmationbücher)

In both the Catholic and the Lutheran churches, most children were between thirteen and twenty when they were confirmed. The confirmation record gives the child's name and place and date of birth; the name and occupation of the father; and—quite often—the later marriage of the child. These records are either in the original churches or in the church archives.

There is one problem you should consider in connection with church records. If you know the religion of your ancestor but have problems with the location of his or her birthplace because you discover a number of places in Germany with the same name, you may find some help in knowing which religion was predominant in certain areas.

For example, let us suppose you know your Catholic ancestor came from a place named Schwarzenberg. You find there is one place with that name in Hesse (Hessen), one in Brandenburg, one in Prussia (Preussen), and one in Bavaria (Bayern). The odds are that the place you want is in Bavaria, because Brandenburg and Prussia are mainly Lutheran, and Hesse is Protestant but not necessarily Lutheran. This is not an infallible method, but it may help.

The other problem that may cause you difficulty, particularly in Schleswig-Holstein and Friesland, is different naming practices. Farms carried a name, usually the one given to them by the original owner. The name stayed with the farm even when the ownership changed. The trouble is that when a new owner bought the farm he would take its name as his own or, if a man's wife inherited a farm, he would change his name to her maiden name. This could produce the complication of children bearing different surnames within the same family. If you run into this problem, find out if the confirmation books are available for the particular parish, because these records usually give the original name and the later one.

CHAPTER 6:
IMMIGRATION

IMMIGRATION TO THE UNITED STATES

Although the major period of German immigration into North America was in the nineteenth century, the first mass entry of German colonists was in 1683 when Germantown, in Pennsylvania, was founded. Even so, the description "mass" is a misnomer, since the party totaled thirteen families. However, it is easier to use the word "mass" to describe organized bodies of immigrants as opposed to the scattered entry of individuals or small family groups. It is quite possible that individual Germans landed before 1683, but we have no certain record of their arrival, although rumor has it that the earliest German settlers were in Virginia and Maryland as early as 1608.

From the early eighteenth century to the nineteenth century Germans settled in many states besides the three I have mentioned above—notably New York, the Carolinas, Texas, Wisconsin, Ohio, and Illinois. In this brief account of German immigration, we must confine ourselves to major areas of settlement rather than attempting a complete history of all fifty states, or even those in the original thirteen colonies.

German settlement really commenced with the arrival of the "Palatines" in 1709 and their settlement in the colony of New York. Although the description "Palatine" actually applied only to people from the Palatinate area of the Rhineland (now known as the state or land of Rheinland-Pfalz), it was also used to describe people from Baden, Bavaria (Bayern), Alsace (Elsass), Hesse (Hessen), and Württemberg.

There were a number of reasons for the great migrations—poor crops, bad winters, heavy taxes, military service, religious persecution, and most of all, the devastation caused by the Thirty Years War (1618–1648) and subsequent invasions of the Rhineland by France in 1673, 1688, and

1707. The winter of 1708–09 was the worst in Europe in more than a century. The intense cold started in October and continued until the end of April, and the vines and fruit trees in the southwest of the German area were destroyed. According to contemporary accounts, birds died in the air and spittle leaving the mouth was ice before it reached the ground. The disaster was total and the future without hope.

The Palatines started to arrive in London, England, via Rotterdam in 1708, and in 1709, according to some reports, 30,000 arrived between May and October. The refugees arriving in England had every intention of continuing their journey as soon as possible to Pennsylvania and the Carolinas. Representatives of these colonies had been active in the Rhineland proclaiming the attractions of good land and low taxes. William Penn himself paid several visits to the area, and in 1681 leaflets were distributed offering land in Pennsylvania at the price of two English pounds for 100 acres.

However, the English government, faced with a multitude of refugees beyond all expectations, blew hot and cold on the project. Objections were raised by English settlers already in the colonies and efforts were made to arrange settlement on various islands in the Caribbean, in England itself, and in Ireland. Meanwhile, the Palatines continued to pour into London, and tented camps were set up in the suburbs, and houses, barns, and warehouses were requisitioned or donated.

Eventually some 3,000 Protestants were persuaded to settle in Ireland, where the policy of the English government was to dispossess the Catholic peasants and replace them with Protestants. By January 1710 more than 2,000 of the original 3,000 had settled in Co. Limerick and Co. Dublin, but another thousand had returned to London. Those remaining were given eight acres of land for every member of the family.

The great John Wesley, founder of the religious movement that bears his name, visited a Palatine community in Co. Limerick in 1760. He records in his journal: "I rode over to Killiheen, a German settlement, nearly twenty miles south of Limerick. In the evening I preached to another colony of Germans at Ballygarane. The third is at Court Mattrass, a mile from Killiheen. There is no cursing or swearing, no Sabbath-breaking, no drunkenness, no ale-house in any of them. How will these poor foreigners rise up in the judgement against those that are round about them." In spite of their difficulties, they survived, and there are many descendants in the area today with names like Switzer, Heck, Miller, and Shire.

Meanwhile, those left in London were living under very poor conditions—financial aid from the English government was minimal, but it was augmented by private donations obtained by the efforts of the

Church of England. Inevitably, the refugees were accused of becoming a financial burden, of taking jobs away from the English, and even of introducing the plague into the country. Several of the camps and settlements were attacked by the London mobs and a number of Palatines were killed or wounded.

The leader of the first contingent to arrive in 1708 was the Rev. Joshua Kocherthal. His party consisted of forty-one people from Landau, in the Palatinate, and fourteen more from the same place joined them a few weeks later. It was eventually decided they should settle on the Hudson River, in the New York colony, some fifty miles north of New York City. They sailed in mid-October 1708 and took nine weeks on the voyage. Their settlement was named Newburgh.

By mid-summer of 1709 the Palatines were arriving at Rotterdam at the rate of a thousand a week. From there they were shipped to England in transport ships that had brought soldiers over to the Netherlands to fight in the War of the Spanish Succession. In September the English became worried about the number of Catholics among the refugees, and some 3,000 were sent back to the Rhineland with a parting gift of five Dutch guilders.

In January 1710 the first mass sailing to the New World took place—some 600 Palatines left for the Carolinas and later founded the settlement of New Bern. Three thousand more sailed for New York in April. Eighteen hundred of them settled on the Hudson some ninety miles north of the city, while the balance stayed in the city itself. In 1712 the financial subsidies from the colonial government to the Hudson River settlers were abruptly ended. They were told they could hire themselves out as servants in New York or New Jersey but nowhere else. During the next five years many of them crossed into Pennsylvania, while others settled in Albany, Schenectady, and in Schoharie, on the Mohawk.

From 1717 onward there was a steady stream of settlers into Pennsylvania, both from New York and directly from England. Many settlements were established in the eastern part of the colony between the Susquehanna and Delaware rivers and around the fast-growing city of Philadelphia. Pennsylvania was "the promised land" for the Germans—both those waiting in England and those now sailing directly from European ports. There were liberal terms for land purchase, religious toleration, and the existence of established German settlements and a way of life that made the colony irresistible.

Between 1727 and 1775 nearly 70,000 Germans went to Pennsylvania. A little earlier—in 1710—they had begun to enter Maryland in large numbers, and by 1756 the majority of the population was estimated to be of German origin. The main cause of this sudden departure from Pennsylvania was Indian attacks on the isolated German settlements and the refusal of the Quaker government to provide firearms for their protection. The main area of settlement was around Frederick and along the Monocacy River. At about the same time (1709–1729), small settlements were also established in Virginia and North Carolina. It is estimated that 200,000 Germans immigrated to North America in the eighteenth century and more than three million in the nineteenth. At the time of the Revolution nearly ten percent of the population was of German origin. German came close to being declared the official language in Pennsylvania.

Immigration tapered off toward the end of the eighteenth century because of industrialization in the German areas of Europe and consequent increased prosperity. There were also official restrictions on emigration in many of the states that were later to form the unified country of Germany, and an increase in compulsory military service. However, the pause was short-lived. By 1818 one bad harvest had followed another, the Napoleonic Wars had taken their toll of life and property, and religious disputes within the Lutheran Church had led to ill feeling and a disruption of orderly life. All these events led to another wave of emigration—this time from Bavaria (Bayern) and Württemberg, and later from Hesse (Hessen), Thuringia (Thüringen), and West Prussia (Westpreussen). By 1840 all the Germanic areas were contributing to the floodtide, but the majority still came from the southwest—mainly because of the history of close association with America and family connections with those already established in the great republic beyond the ocean.

The religious disputes I mentioned above were caused in the main by a compulsory union of the Reformed and Lutheran churches ordered by King Frederick William III of Prussia. A breakaway sect opposed to the union and known as the "Old Lutherans" took the lead in the new emigration. More than a thousand went to the United States in 1839—700 to Wisconsin and the rest to Buffalo. In 1847 a large organized party left Lippe-Detmold in the North Rhineland for Missouri and Wisconsin, and in the following year more Missouri settlements were established by immigrants from Westphalia (Westfalen) and Hamburg. Smaller family groups went to the cities of Milwaukee and Cleveland.

At this time many Germans who were destitute had their passage overseas paid by their local community to save the increasing costs to the public purse. In the early 1840s a number of emigrant societies (generally known as Auswanderungsverein) were set up in various parts of the German area. They were organized on a cooperative self-help basis with the support of the various state governments. Their objectives were to help members emigrate, and this help included both money and advice. The records of many of these societies—but by no means all—are in the state or city archives in Germany, together with copies of early newspapers devoted to the subject of emigration. The main centers were in the following places (the name of the existing state is given in parentheses):

Berlin
Breslau (now Wrocław, in Poland)
Darmstadt (Hessen)
Düsseldorf (Nordrhein-Westfalen)
Frankfurt-am-Main (Hessen) Giessen (Hessen)
Hannover (Niedersachsen)
Karlsruhe (Baden-Württemberg)
Leipzig (Sachsen)
Mainz (Rheinland-Pfalz)
Stuttgart (Baden-Württemberg)

The high points in immigration into the United States in the nineteenth century were in 1854 when more than a quarter of a million Germans arrived, and in the period 1866–1873. The latter years saw the emergence of Prussia (Preussen) as the dominant state in the German area and a series of wars against Austria, Denmark, and France, culminating in the proclamation of the German Empire in 1870. In 1880 more than 200,000 Germans immigrated to North America. The estimates—and they can be no more than that—are that between 1820 and 1900 the number of immigrants totaled between three and five million.

Since those days there has been a steady flow of German immigrants, but not on the same scale. The end of constant wars between the various states, the unification of Germany, and the end of cheap land in the United States all made the Fatherland a more attractive place in which to live, and this was reflected in smaller immigration figures. In 1900 the annual total was down to 20,000.

As you are of German descent you should always remember that your ancestor may have settled in the United States after a brief stay in Canada, or he may have emigrated from the United States to Canada. Among many early Mennonite settlers there was a great deal of movement backward and forward across an unsupervised and unregulated border, and also many arranged marriages between a man settled in Ontario, Canada, and a woman in Pennsylvania or New York—or vice versa.

If you are not of Mennonite descent, then you may still come into cross-border problems because of the close friendship of Lutheran families in the two countries. An additional problem may possibly stem from a descent from one of the "Hessians"—the soldiers from the German area of Europe who fought in the British army during the American Revolution. The term "Hessian" is a misnomer. In fact, the German mercenaries came from many places in the Germanic area besides Hesse. They came from Brunswick, Anhalt-Zerbst, Anspach-Bayreuth, Prussia,

Württemberg, and in fact from many other areas of Europe, including Austria, Estonia, Latvia, Hungary, and Italy.

After the United States became independent, the German soldiers went their separate ways—some went back to their homes in Europe, some stayed in the United States, and many others crossed the border into Canada (see below). Because of this general dispersal, it has always been difficult to arrive at an estimate of their numbers.

IMMIGRATION TO CANADA

The number of German settlers in Canada was minute compared with the number in the United States, and settlement was confined to two provinces in the early days—Ontario and Nova Scotia. However, many of the Germans in Canada maintained close family and religious ties with German settlers in Pennsylvania and Maryland, and to discover more about your German ancestors in the United States, you may find you need to do some of your research in Canada.

German settlers first entered the province of Ontario (then named Upper Canada) from Pennsylvania in about 1786, but there was no mass movement, and during the next twenty-one years only twenty-five families settled in the southwestern area of the province—in what is now the city of Kitchener and the county of Waterloo. Many more followed in 1807 as land in Pennsylvania became too costly and frequent subdivision of farms within families reduced agricultural productivity. A German company was formed in Canada to promote immigration from Pennsylvania, primarily among Mennonites. An option was taken on 60,000 acres in 1803, and the purchase money of $40,000 was raised in the United States, mainly from Pennsylvania's Franklin County. A further 45,000 acres was bought a short time afterward. In those early days all the Germans in Canada were related to families south of the border.

The settlers came from Franklin, Lancaster, Montgomery, and Bucks counties—particularly the townships of Bedminster, Hillborn, Plumstead, and Tinicum. Many of them were descended from Swiss-German Mennonites. The settlement area in Ontario was an isolated one beyond the districts officially opened by the government, and the Germans lived very self-contained lives. They shared a common language and customs and were bound together by the Mennonite religion. The steady influx from Pennsylvania ended by 1828 but was preceded in the early 1820s by a large number of arrivals—known as "Reichsdeutsche"—coming directly from Germany through the port of Halifax. The other source of German settlement in scattered areas of Canada was that of the Hessians—mercenaries who had served with the British forces during the Revolutionary War. When the British were defeated and the United States created, the Hessians came north into Canada and received grants of land from the British government, mainly along the northern shores of Lake Ontario. It seems likely that at least 10,000 Hessians settled in Canada. There is one story that in the period 1783–1793 they constituted ten percent of the marriageable male population of Québec; however, I find this high figure a little difficult to credit in view of the high birth rate of the Québecois and the population of the province at that time.

On their arrival in Canada they joined other German soldiers who had done their military service in Canada without crossing the border. The latter also qualified for the land grants. To further complicate matters, many of these "Canadian" Germans migrated south to the United States a few years later, and others returned to Europe.

Virginia DeMarce, in her book *German Military Settlers in Canada After the American Revolution* (see Bibliography), lists some 2,500 names. A few entries taken at random show the valuable genealogical information she has researched so painstakingly:

ABRAHAM Daniel. Brunswick troops. Born Schorborn, aged 36 years 11 months, discharged in Canada 1783. Marysburgh, Ontario.

DUDLOFF, Gotlieb. Surgeon's mate. Regt. of Specht. Born Erich-swalde, Saxony. Aged 28 years 7 months.

RAUCH, Joseph. Brunswick troops. Born Innsbruck. Aged 45. Dis-charged in Canada 1783.

SCHAEFFER, Andreas. Regiment de Barner. Born Kies, Wurzburg. Aged 29. Discharged Canada 1783.

SCHMIDT, Jacque. Private Corps Company. Hesse-Hanau Infantry. Discharged 1783. Born Bellersdorf. Aged 34.

There is more information to be found in the LDS Church records, in Library and Archives Canada in Ottawa, and in the provincial archives of the three provinces of Ontario, Nova Scotia, and Québec.

The major and much more important German settlement was in the southwest part of the province of Upper Canada, and this we will talk about first, returning later to Nova Scotia.

The German area in Waterloo County was first known as Ebytown—named after an early Mennonite bishop, Benjamin Eby—and later as Sandhills and Berlin. The changes in immigration sources at this time—the early 1820s—led to important changes in the life of the area. The Mennonite farmers soon found themselves in a minority position as the later arrivals were primarily Lutheran and Moravian and were more interested in trade and manufacturing than they were in agriculture. By 1833 the words "Made in Berlin" on manufactured goods demonstrated the industrial growth of the area. It was true that good land could still be bought for two dollars an acre in the townships around Berlin such as Wilmot, Woolwich, and Wellesley, and there was still a steady drift north from Pennsylvania, but it was on a very small scale.

By the mid-1830s immigrants were coming to Berlin from all parts of the German area of Europe—Baden, Bayern (Bavaria), Hessen-Darmstadt, Elsass-Lothringen (Alsace-Lorraine), Holstein, Mecklenburg, Württemberg, and even from the German settlements in the Baltic areas of Estonia, Latvia, and Lithuania. No single religious group was predominant—by 1835 the Lutherans, Moravians, Baptists, and Swedenborgians had churches in the area, and by 1850 the Catholics. By this time more than 12,000 Germans had settled in Upper Canada.

In 1857 the Grand Trunk Railway had reached Berlin and the immigrants landing at Québec were able to travel directly to their destination by train. On one day in that year, ninety German immigrants arrived in Berlin and thus increased the population by one percent in one day. Most of these newcomers were from Mecklenburg.

In 1916—in the middle of World War I—it was decided, as the result of a plebiscite, to change the name of Berlin to Kitchener. The new name was a tribute to the memory of a British general who had drowned earlier in the year when a battleship on which he was traveling had been torpedoed by a German submarine.

The German influence in Kitchener, and in Waterloo County, is strong and the history of the founding families is well documented. There are many instances where ancestor-hunters of Pennsylvania-German descent have found out more about their ancestry in Kitchener than in Philadelphia or Harrisburg! There are a great many family histories, both published and in manuscript form, in the Grace Schmidt Room of the Kitchener Public Library (85 Queen Street North, Kitchener, Ontario N2H 2H1; phone: 519-743-0271; website: www.kpl.org/) and at Conrad Grebel University College in the University of Waterloo (140 Westmount Road North, Waterloo, Ontario N2L 3G6; website: http://grebel.uwaterloo.ca/). The latter has a large collection of Mennonite records but not a great many church registers. It must always be remembered, of course, that the Mennonites practiced adult baptism, as did the Baptists.

There are many Mennonite sects in Ontario that do not deposit their records at the university, and you will have a difficult time in tracing their whereabouts. The Old Order Amish keep their genealogical records in the Amish Heritage Historical Library, RR4 Aylmer, Ontario N5H 2R3, but the following sects retain their records: Old Order Mennonite; Beachy Amish Mennonite; Old Colony Mennonite; Conservative Mennonite; Reformed Mennonite; Church of God in Christ, Mennonite; Evangelical Mennonite Mission; and Mennonite Brethren. However, most of the records of the original group of settlers from Pennsylvania are at the University of Waterloo (see previous page).

Now let us turn to German settlement in the province of Nova Scotia. There is no connection between settlers there and those in Pennsylvania, except in a few isolated cases. The 3,000 Germans who settled in the province came directly from the German area of Europe, almost entirely by direct passage from the port of Rotterdam in the Netherlands to the port of Halifax, Nova Scotia. Settlement on an organized scale started in the mid-1700s when the British government was encouraging Protestant immigration into Canada. In the main, these Germans came from Baden, Hessen, Württemberg, and Rheinland-Pfalz, plus there were a few Swiss-Germans. Some twelve ships carried immigrants to Nova Scotia in the 1750s, and the passenger lists of ten of them have been researched and published by Terrence Punch, Nova Scotia's leading expert on German immigration into the province. Later in the century there was some settlement by the Hessian mercenaries whom I mentioned earlier.

The Germans in Nova Scotia settled mainly in the area of Lunenberg in 1753, but later moved into other places in this small province. There are a number of books about German settlement in Nova Scotia listed in the Bibliography.

PASSENGER LISTS

In most countries these are either nonexistent or so few in relation to the whole that they need not be considered as a source of genealogical information. In Germany, however, the story is very different, and that is why I put them second to church registers as a good source of information. In fact, they are equally vital to people whose ancestors came from many other countries in Europe—Austria, Bulgaria, the former Czechoslovakia, Hungary, Poland, Romania, Serbia, the Scandinavian countries, and the former USSR.

Bremen and Hamburg were the main ports for European emigration from 1832 (Bremen) and 1845 (Hamburg) up to 1934. Unfortunately, most of the Bremen lists were destroyed, except those after 1920, but the Hamburg lists from 1850 to 1934 (with the exception of January to June 1853 and August 1914 to 1919), which contain the names of over five million people who emigrated through the port, are available online at **www.ancestry.com** (payment required) and on microfilm from the LDS Family History Library. They can also be viewed at a facility in Hamburg called Port of Dreams–Emigrant World BallinStadt (Veddeler Bogen 2, 20539 Hamburg; phone: 011-49-40-319-791-60; e-mail: info@ballinstadt.de; website: www.ballinstadt.de/), which has special exhibition areas, a public research section with computer workstations for visitors interested in tracing the emigration history of their ancestors, and staff members who are specially trained in genealogy and are available to provide assistance. In its in-house research center, not only can you search the Hamburg Passenger Lists, you also have access to the world's largest genealogical database, including U.S. censuses and address books.

The passenger lists are divided into direct and indirect records. Most emigrants traveled *directly* to a port in their new homeland. For example, the great majority of immigrants to the United States landed in New York; from there they scattered across the country and to Canada and South America. You will not need to search the lists, of course, if you already know the place of origin of your emigrating ancestor, and the details of his or her family.

The Bremen lists started in 1832, but lists from 1875–1908 older than three years were destroyed due to lack of space in the Bremen Archives. With the exception of 3,017 passenger lists for the years 1920–1939, all other lists were lost in World War II. The surviving lists have been transcribed in a joint project between the Bremen Chamber of Congress and the Bremen Society for Genealogical Investigation (Die Maus), and they are now available online at **www.passengerlists.de**/. In addition, a list of emigrants who sailed from Bremen to New York was compiled from U.S. sources by Gary J. Zimmerman and Marion Wolfert. Some 132,000 names for the period 1847–1871 were collected and published (see Bibliography). You will also find online lists, transcribed from National Archives microfilms, of passengers from Bremen to New York and Bremen to Baltimore.

Besides Hamburg and Bremen, there were several other major ports of departure, and a number of small harbors such as Danzig (Gdańsk), Lübeck, Rostock, and Stettin saw emigrant departures. Practically no records exist of passengers leaving the smaller ports, but lists are available in various places for some of the main ports, and in most cases copies have been made by the LDS Church. These ports are listed below with the location of the archives containing the records where they still exist:

Göteborg (1869-1951), Landsarkivet, P.O. Box 19035, 400 12 Göteborg, Sweden; website: http://riksarkivet.se/goteborg. The Family History Library has indexes on microfilm, and the lists are searchable on Ancestry.com.

Antwerp (1855), Rjksarchief Beveren, Kruibekesteenweg 39/1, 9120 Beveren; website: http://arch.arch.be/. Only one passenger register survived WWI (the one for 1855); some incomplete passenger lists exist for the period 1920–1940.

Le Havre (1749–1830), Archives départmentales de Seine-Maritime, Hôtel du département, Quai Jean Moulin CS 56101, 76101 Rouen cedex, France; website: www.archivesdepartementales76.net/.

Bordeaux (1713–1787), Archives départementales de la Gironde, 72-78 cours Balguerie Stuttenberg, 33300 Bordeaux, France; website: http://archives.cg33.fr/.

It must be pointed out that the passenger lists in the various ports mentioned above have not all been indexed, and in order to obtain details it may be necessary to provide the name of the ship and the date of sailing. Check **https://familysearch.org** to see what lists are available on microfilm at the Family History Library.

The main United States ports used by immigrants from Europe were New York, Philadelphia, Boston, Baltimore, and New Orleans. Some passenger lists for these ports do exist. More information can be obtained from the National Archives in Washington and its regional archives. You can find a list of U.S. ports of arrival and their available passenger lists 1820–1957 at **www.genesearch.com/ports.html**.

It is important to remember that the place of origin shown in the passenger lists is not always the birthplace. However, in that case the odds are that the place of birth was quite near the place of domicile. For example, your ancestor may be shown as coming from Herrenhäusen (a small city), whereas his place of birth may have been Neuburg, a little village a few miles away.

If you are consulting passenger lists, the following glossary may be of help to you:

Alter	Age
Anschrift	Address
Auswanderer	Emigrant
Beruf	Occupation
Bestimmungsort	Destination
Datum	Date
Erwachsen	Adult
Geboren	Born
Geburtsort	Birthplace
Gewerbe	Occupation
Herkunftsort	Place of origin
Kinder	Children
Länder	Provinces or states
Ledig	Single
Namen	Names
Nationalität	Nationality
Ort	Place

Strasse	Street
Verheiratet	Married
Vorname	Given name
Wohin	Destination
Zuname	Surname

Several of the German states kept their own records of emigration from the state, notably Brunswick (Braunschweig), Hesse (Hessen), and Württemberg. Other similar records were kept in many individual cities and towns. Some of these records are now searchable online—links to these are found at **www.germanroots.com/emigration.html**. Some German archives have posted lists of emigrants online as well. For example, emigrants from Baden, Wuerttemberg, and Hohenzollern are online at **www.auswanderer-bw.de/**; the website **http:/aidaonline. niedersachsen.de/** lists emigrants from Hannover, Braunschweig, and Oldenburg; and **www.lippe-auswanderer.de/** lists emigrants from Lippe.

Other possible sources of information are the official lists of permits to emigrate. Most of these have been lost, but some have been published for the areas of Brunswick (Braunschweig), Nassau, Sachsen-Weimar, and Waldeck. The German Genealogical Society of America has copies of these.

Another source of information about arrivals in the United States from the Germanic areas of Europe is a multi-volume work called *Germans to America: Lists of Passengers Arriving at U.S. Ports*, edited by Ira A. Glazier and P. William Filby (see Bibliography).

In August 2005 a museum opened on the New Harbor in Bremerhaven where, between 1852 and 1890, almost 1.2 million people left for the New World. The German Emigration Center—the winner of the prestigious European Museum of the Year Award for 2007—contains an extensive library with more than 2,000 volumes on the topic of emigration, as well as a continually growing collection of photographs, biographies, documents, and databases that might help you research ancestors who immigrated to the United States. In April 2012 the German Emigration Center opened its new extension wing, which focuses on the history of Germany as a country of immigration.

Here is the contact information:

German Emigration Center
Columbusstrasse 65
27568 Bremerhaven
Phone: 011-49-471-90-22-00. Fax: 011-49-471-90-22-022
E-mail: info@dah-bremerhaven.de
Website: www.dah-bremerhaven.de/

Names

In your search of records, remember it was common in the middle 1700s in the Germanic areas to use only the *second* baptismal name in official records in later life. The first name was that of a parent or grandparent and was given as a compliment but never used officially. So Oskar Georg Weber would only appear as Georg Weber.

When researching your ancestors in passenger lists, you must also always be on the lookout for name changes—misspellings, names written as they sounded, names simplified, names changed accidentally or deliberately by immigration officers, names that were anglicized, etc. Here are just a few examples taken at random:

Bekker	Baker	Roth	Ross
Brunn	Brown	Schmitt or	
Heinrich	Henry	Schmidt	Smith
Hellmann	Hill	Schneeburger	Snow
Jong	Young	Stein	Stone
Konig	King	Wasser	Waters
Loewen	Lowe	Werfer	Weaver
Mann	Manning	Werner	Warner
Rickert	Richards		

Finally, while we are on the subject of names, remember diminutives (first names that are shortened) or "pet" names that bear little resemblance to the original. Here are a few examples:

Georg	Yuri, Jorg	Renate	Reni
Heinrich	Henni	Rosina	Sina
Johann	Hansi	Rudolf	Dolf or
Josef	Seppi		Folph
Matthias	Tice	Wilhelm	Villie
Philip	Lipsi		

CHAPTER 7:
VITAL AND OTHER RECORDS

Civil Registration (Reichspersonenstandsgesetz)

This started in 1875 following the unification of Germany, but only so far as the main Germanic area was concerned. In some areas the system had started earlier. There is a Register Office (Standesamt) for each particular area. All records of births, marriages, and deaths are kept there, but a duplicate of each entry is sent to the state capital. It should be noted that a registration area can be quite large, covering several towns and villages.

In those areas originally under French control, such as Alsace-Lorraine (Elsass-Lothringen) and a few other small areas west of the Rhine, registration started in 1810; in Frankfurt (once a Free City) it began in 1850, in Lübeck and Oldenburg in 1811, in Hanover (Hannover) in 1809, and in most parts of Prussia (Preussen) in about 1870. The death registers are particularly useful because they very often give not only the place and date of death but also the names of the parents of the deceased and any surviving children.

In 2009 Germany relaxed its rights-to-privacy laws, making civil registration records more accessible. Birth records are now available after 110 years, marriage records after 80 years, and death records after 30 years, so long as all persons mentioned in the record are deceased. In addition, under the new law older records will be transferred from the local civil registration office to an archive, making access easier.

Wills (Testamente)

The probate system in Germany is a little complicated. Once a lawyer has drawn up a will, a copy is deposited in the district courthouse (Amtsgericht) for the area in which the testator is *living*. The local authorities then notify the Civil Register Office (Standesamt) in the district where the testator was *born*. When he dies, the Standesamt in his place of death notifies the Standesamt in his place of birth, and the latter, in turn, notifies the Court of Law of the location of the will. The court then executes the will. Original wills are either in the district courthouse or in the state archives (Staatsarchiv) in each province.

Censuses (Volkszählungen)

These have been held on a countrywide basis since 1871, with the first large-scale census taking place in 1895, but others were held at irregular intervals in various areas. However, many censuses did not survive World War II, and generally only the compiled statistical information that was gathered from the censuses is available, so they are not of great use to genealogists.

GERMANY: 1871, 1880, 1885, 1890, 1895, 1900, 1905, 1910, 1919, 1925, 1933, 1939

WEST GERMANY: 1946, 1950, 1961, 1970, 1987

EAST GERMANY: 1946, 1964, 1971, 1981

BADEN: 1852, 1855, 1858, 1861, 1867, 1925, 1933, 1946

BADEN-WÜRTTEMBERG: 1946, 1950, 1961, 1970

BAYERN (BAVARIA): 1846, 1849, 1852, 1855, 1858, 1861, 1867, 1946, 1950, 1961, 1970

BERLIN (WEST): 1945, 1946, 1950, 1961, 1970

BERLIN (EAST): 1945, 1946, 1964

BREMEN: 1900, 1905, 1946, 1950, 1961, 1970

DRESDEN: 1871

HAMBURG: 1866, 1867, 1871, 1946, 1950, 1961, 1970

HESSEN (HESSE): 1925, 1946, 1950, 1961, 1970

KÖLN (COLOGNE): 1961

NORDRHEIN-WESTFALEN (NORTH RHINE-WESTPHALIA): 1946, 1950, 1961, 1970

PREUSSEN (PRUSSIA): 1895, 1900, 1905, 1910

RHEINLAND-PFALZ (RHINELAND-PALATINATE): 1946, 1950, 1961, 1970

SAARLAND: 1927, 1935, 1961, 1970 (see under France for 1945–57)

SCHLESWIG-HOLSTEIN: 1803, 1835, 1840, 1855, 1860, 1946, 1950, 1961, 1970

WÜRTTEMBERG: 1821, 1832, 1843, 1846, 1849, 1852, 1855, 1858, 1861, 1867, 1946, 1950

DEUTSCHER ZOLLVEREIN: 1855 (This was the area included in a Customs Union of North German States.)

Census records of some provinces or towns may be accessible at various archives, but you'd have to hunt around to find ones that are available to researchers. Check with the municipal archives (Stadtarchiv) or the Civil Register Office (Standesamt) in each city or district to see if any records are available. There is an ongoing project to post census records from Schleswig-Holstein online; see **www.aggsh.de/engl/pag/ vz-pub.htm**. Some Mecklenburg-Schwerin censuses are searchable online at **www.ancestry.com**.

The census returns of several areas have been copied by the LDS Church and are available at the Family History Library. The 1819 census of Mecklenburg-Schwerin is one of the most significant at the library, since the complete census survived and information in the census includes name, gender, birth date, place of birth, marital status, occupation, and religion. Various census records for Schleswig-Holstein are also among those available at the library.

East Germany, when it was independent, destroyed its census returns after counting.

Police Registration (Einwohnermelderegister)

This started in most of the states about 1840 and controlled internal movement. The records included full name, family details, date and place of birth, and occupation. You will usually be able to locate these police registration records in local archives, police headquarters, or state archives.

Military Records (Kriegslisten)

These are incomplete and not always easily accessible but they are worth working on because every male was liable for military service in the various state armies. If your ancestors came from the Schleswig-Holstein area, you are luckier than most. The system there involved the registration of every male child at birth, and the record was kept up-to-date as far as addresses were concerned until his call-up date. A good sequence of discoveries can follow: If you find your ancestor's addresses from the military records, you can trace the census returns; if you find the census returns you find the place of birth; if you find the place of birth you find the church records, you lucky people from Schleswig-Holstein! The military lists in general date back to the early 1700s and are in the state archives.

Certificate of Birth (Geburtszeugnis or Geburtsbrief)

When a person wanted to establish citizenship in a city or town, or get married, or join a guild (see next page), he or she would have to produce this document. The individual had to produce a letter from the priest or pastor in his or her birthplace and the civil authorities would then issue the certificate.

Guild Records (Gilderbücher)

These can provide valuable information for you. The guild (like the trade union of today) was powerful in the work field. It permitted its members to work only at a particular trade, in a particular place. It made sure that a newcomer in town became a citizen before he joined the guild. Remember that being an inhabitant was not the same as being a citizen. Anyone could be an inhabitant, but you had to earn the right to become a citizen. You had to work hard, not be a charge on the community, not be a bastard, be sober, be a churchgoer, and know the right people.

Then, and only then, the good citizen could apply to join a guild, and the guild records show his name, his trade, the names of his wife and children, the date and place of his birth, the date and place of his marriage, and the date of his arrival in the city and his entry into the guild. The guilds exercised so much control over their members that they could dictate the area of the city in which they lived, and even whom they married (preferably the daughter of another guild member).

The guild records are either in local archives or in state archives, and they date back in many cases to the early seventeenth century, and in a few instances even earlier.

Newspapers

German-language newspapers are rich sources of information for genealogical researchers. They include notices of births, baptisms, marriages, and deaths; notices of intent to emigrate; trade news; appointments to office; and much more. Approximately 2,000 historic German-language newspapers are now online. The German-North American Research Partnership has compiled an online index to historic German-language newspaper access, which includes German-language newspapers regardless of geographic location. It can be viewed at **http://wessweb.info/index. php/German-Language_Newspaper_Access_in_North_America**. In addition, Ernest Thode's *Historic German Newspapers Online* (see Bibliography) is a useful guide to historic newspapers online—most of which are from Germany and the former Austro-Hungarian Empire.

Other Available Records

There are three important sources of information in Germany that are often overlooked. They are, in order of value, Ortssippenbücher (Local Family Books), Geschlechterbücher (Lineage Books), and Leichenpredigten (Funeral Sermons).

These records should be used in conjunction with all the other sources I have listed; none of them, on their own, will provide you with all the answers, but they may well fill gaps, solve relationship puzzles, and give you the place of origin, marriage, or death of a particular ancestor. Unfortunately, the records I mention are not in any one place, nor are the locations listed. You will have to write to the particular place or general area in which you are interested: to the Mayor (Bürgermeister) for a village, town, or city; or to the local Catholic priest or Lutheran minister; or to the director of the city archives (Stadtsarchiv) or the provincial archives (Landesarchiv or Staatsarchiv). You will have to ferret out the locations for yourself, but I never promised you a Rosengarten!

Local Family Books (Ortssippenbücher)

German genealogists and sociologists have been very interested since the early part of this century in studying the various families living in a particular area. This is partly pure research, partly love of history, and partly the German passion for tidiness, for having everything in its proper place. The Ortssippenbuch for a particular area will list all the members of every family (living and dead) and their relationship with each other. The source of the information was, of course, the church register, both Lutheran and Catholic.

As interest in the projects grew, the organization of them was taken over by a branch of the government, and as each district was completed, the results were published in book form. The ultimate aim was to have a genealogical record of the entire German people.

This was a point where the interests of genealogists in tracing family descent coincided with the National Socialist racial policies for a brief period. After 1933 many German citizens, particularly farmers, storeowners, and teachers, were required to provide a certificate proving their Aryan descent—der Ahnennachweis, as it was called—and the existence of a completed Ortssippenbuch for their district simplified their task. The tracing of lineage was required back to the early nineteenth century; only the S.S. demanded lineage back to 1750 for their members.

Publication was suspended in 1940; after the war the task was taken over by the genealogical organizations without regard to any racial purity, and today some 150 books are in print. In addition, very many books were started and never finished, or finished and never printed. You will find the books or manuscripts in local and state archives. The present-day compiling of the books is not being done on a very even basis, since it depends very much on the energy and dedication of the various genealogical organizations. About half of the completed books refer to districts in the Länder of Baden and Hessen-Nassau.

A list compiled in 1997 of existing Ortssippenbucher is available online at **www.genealogienetz.de/faqs/ortsbuch**.

German Lineage Books (Deutsche Geschlechterbücher)

These books date back in some cases to the late eighteenth century when the first known one was published. The contents, of course, go back very much further. They contain the details of descent of bourgeois families, i.e. middle class and lower upper class, not the nobility. Each book contains a number of family trees of various German families. They are on a regional basis in that all the families in the book are from one district.

Some 200 of the Geschlechterbücher have been published, and more are on the way. Each family section starts with the earliest known member and descends through the years to the date of publication. It also lists occupations, and places of baptism, marriage, death, and residence. Some are viewable online at **http://archive.org/search.php?query=deutsches%20geschlechterbuch.**

The LDS Family History Library has all but a few volumes in its collection. These volumes often give many generations of German families. They are indexed at the end of each volume, and the first 150 volumes are indexed in a cumulative index called *Stammfolgen-Verzeichnisse für das genealogische Handbuch des Adels und das deutsche Geschlechterbuch*, which is also available at the Family History Library, as is a filmed copy of the 1963 index for volumes 1–134.

Funeral Sermons (Leichenpredigten)

This source of genealogical information is almost unique to Germany, but I have found similar records in Hungary. They originated in the sixteenth century for a rather odd reason. When the Reformation reached Germany it meant the end of a very ornate and impressive funeral mass in the Catholic Church. This was a great occasion in which the deceased was praised at length by a local orator (often a professional, paid for his services), a large choir performed, and a sermon was delivered by the local priest (or by the bishop if the dead man or woman was important enough, or if the remaining spouse was generous to the church).

The end of this kind of ceremony left a gap in the lives of many people, mainly among Lutherans and Calvinists. They had embraced a simple and stark religion, but many of them missed a good funeral mass! So the funeral sermon was born and took the form of a eulogy at the graveside. Some sermons were entirely religious in content, but many were biographical and recounted the whole life of the deceased with details of births, marriages, public or military service, and other events of note.

After the ceremony the sermons were printed and circulated to all the friends of the family. There are well over 100,000 of these preserved in various locations and covering the period from about 1550 up to around

1800. Some of them are only a page or two in length, but some, if the deceased was famous, run to a hundred pages or more!

You can usually depend on the information contained in them being accurate; since the sermon was to be circulated among family and friends, there was no point in lying or exaggerating the life and accomplishments of the deceased. Obviously, certain events would probably be quietly ignored: a period of insanity, a bastard child, dishonorable discharge from the army, a conviction for theft—that sort of thing would be left unsaid.

You can see that these three sources may well be of great value to you. Remember, though, that two of them are limited in their scope. The Lineage Books are confined to the bourgeois families, the Funeral Sermons to the wealthier Protestants, and only the local Family Books record everybody, Catholic and Lutheran, rich and poor, in fact all classes of society.

There are still more available records of use to you. In some localities you will find all of them, in others only one or two:

	Approximate starting date
Adressbuch (City Directory)	1750*
Bürgerbuch (Citizenship Record)	1300
Familienregister (Family Registers)	1800
Gerichtsprotokolle (Court Records)	1500*
Grundbücher (Land Records)	1000*
Lehrlingsbücher (Apprentice Records)	1550
Polizeiregister (Police Registers)	1800
Stadtchroniken (City Chronicles)	1600
Steuerbücher (Tax Records)	1400
Zeitungen (Newspapers)	1800*

The dates are approximate because they vary from province to province, and from city to city. Generally speaking, the records marked with an asterisk are in the provincial archives (Staats- und Landesarchiv) and the others in city archives (Stadtarchiv) or district archives (Kreisarchiv), but there are exceptions to this.

One of the major problems about German records of interest to the ancestor-hunter is that they are scattered among church archives, state archives, city, town, and village archives, some government departments and offices, libraries, and museums. Fortunately, the Internet has made it much easier to locate them, and in some cases to view them. Make no mistake: the material is there; it is available and informative; and it goes back over the centuries. Even minor local events were recorded and will be of interest to you.

CHAPTER 8:
ARCHIVES IN GERMANY

The many divisions of the Germanic area are the cause of the peculiar distribution of archives. From the fourteenth to the nineteenth century, central power over the Germanic lands was exercised by the Hapsburg dynasty, so the central archives of the old Reich are in Vienna (Wien). Since then, the various states have preserved their own archives; as a result, there are archives of all kinds scattered throughout Germany, from major cities down to small villages.

Archives include Staatsarchiv (national), Staatsarchiv (provincial), Landesarchiv (provincial), Stadt (city), Bezirk (district), Dorf (village), Familien (family), Dom (cathedral), Pfarr (parish), Gutsarchiv (property), plus many others for individuals, families, professions, manufacturing plants, religious orders, and youth organizations.

If you visit archives in person you will find they vary greatly—some are beautiful modern buildings, all glass and light, equipped with computers and microfilm readers, with charming, helpful archivists going out of their way to be helpful. Others look like something left over from the Middle Ages, with dusty shelves and even dustier books hidden away in dark corners and illuminated with 40-watt bulbs—presided over by unfriendly archivists who regard their treasures as their own personal property and you as an unwelcome visitor to be gotten rid of as quickly as possible.

It is impossible within the limited space of this book to list all the holdings of each individual archive, although I have done my best to cover all the main sources of information you will find. However, I have discussed the following four German archives in some detail because (a) they may not be as widely known and may be overlooked, and (b) most have material of great value to people whose forebears came from some of the "lost territories" of Germany—Prussia (Ost und West Preussen), Silesia (Schlesien), Posen (Poznań), Pomerania (Pommern), the Sudetenland, Estonia (Estland), and Latvia (Lettland). The latter two countries also include areas that no longer exist as separate entities—Courland (Kurland) and Livländ (Livonia).

Following the descriptions of these four archives, you will find details of many of the archives of value to the ancestor-hunter: a list of the provincial or state archives; a list of local archives alphabetically by city, town, and village; and a list of archives devoted to the papers of noble families.

Herder-Institut
Gisonenweg 5-7
35037 Marburg
Phone: 011-49-6421-184-0. Fax: 011-49-6421-184-139
E-mail: mail@herder-institut.de
Website: www.herder-institut.de/

The Herder-Institut, founded in 1950, is one of Germany's principal centers for historical research on East-Central Europe. As I mentioned earlier, German settlements were established in the Baltic area as early as the time of the Crusades. Over the years the German areas in Estonia and Latvia were almost independent of the host countries. They maintained their language, their social customs, and their religion (mainly Protestant). In 1939 a treaty was signed between the German government and the two Baltic states, in which it was agreed that the records of the German settlements and churches could be filmed. Soon after the work began, the USSR took over the two countries, plus Lithuania, and incorporated them into the Soviet Union. However, the copying of the records continued until 1941. Lithuania was not included in the arrangements as the German areas in that country were practically nonexistent except for Memel.

In Estonia (Estland) a very large part of the material in the State Archives in Tallinn (Reval) and Tartu or Yurev (Dorpat) was copied. This material contains much information about the early German settlements in those areas, and includes records of the University of Dorpat; the city archives of Reval, including lists of citizens and property records; and records of the various craft guilds. The material was transferred to Berlin in 1941 and 1942, and a little later more than 700 rolls were sent to Posen (now Poznań, in Poland) where it was intended that a center for German-Baltic culture would be built after the war. In 1944 the records were transferred to Brunswick (Braunschweig) and came into the custody of the British army a year later. They were kept at Goslar until 1950 and were then transferred to the custody of the Baltic Historical Circle in Göttingen, and finally to the Herder-Institut in 1952.

In Latvia (Lettland) nearly all the German records in the State Archives in Rīga, as well as those in the city archives, were filmed. The latter included the registers of members of the various guilds, rolls of citizens from 1614 to 1812, rent books, land records and deeds, and a variety of other municipal records. From the areas of Latvia known as Courland and Livonia, a number of "Seelenlisten" (church membership rolls) were also filmed, covering a period from the late eighteenth century until the middle of the nineteenth.

The films from Latvia reached the Herder-Institut in the same roundabout way as those from Estonia.

Other miscellaneous records in the Institut include some family papers and family trees from Pomerania (Pommern), extracts from some church books (Kirchenbücher) from the same area—in particular from Schlawe from 1618 to 1710—and a few of these books from Silesia (Schlesien). There are also the family and business papers of Gerhard Lange, from Schlawe, in which he mentions many individuals and families in that area during the last century. Finally, there is a small collection of biographies from the Sudetenland (now in the Czech Republic).

You can access the Archive Database—an online research facility for a part of the holdings of the Herder Institute's document collection—at **www.herder-institut.de/en/service-divisions/document-collection/ archive-database.html**.

The films and manuscripts here, together with other items in the State Archives in Koblenz, form a unique collection of material for German-Baltic research. Some of the records in both locations, including Seelenlisten from Courland (Kurland) and Livonia (Livländ), have been filmed by the LDS Church.

I am sorry I do not have space to list the holdings of the Institute in greater details because it is a treasure-trove of information about the centuries of German occupation of Estonia and Latvia (Livonia and Curland). However, I do suggest you visit their website to check out their listing of holdings.

Evangelisches Zentralarchiv in Berlin (EZA)
Bethaniendamm 29
10997 Berlin
Phone: 011-49-30-22-50-45-20. Fax: 011-49-30-22-50-45-40
E-mail: archiv@ezab.de
Website: www.ezab.de/

One of the great adventure stories of genealogy is that of the successful removal of the great majority of the church registers (Kirchenbücher) of the Evangelical Church from the "lost territories" of Prussia, Posen, Pomerania, and Silesia in 1944 and their eventual safe haven in the central archives of the church in Berlin. These priceless treasures are of great value not only to ancestor-hunters but also to Germans seeking to prove the dates of vital events in order to claim pensions and to obtain passports and inheritances. Almost all of the Kirchenbücher have been microfilmed by the LDS Church (which also played a large part in the preservation of the original registers).

The Evangelical Central Archives in Berlin (EZA) was founded in 1979 as a result of the fusion of the Archives of the Evangelical Church in Germany (Evangelische Kirche in Deutschland) and the Archives of the Evangelical Church of the Prussian Union (Evangelische Kirche der Union).

Its Parish Register Repository contains about 6,000 parish registers from more than 500 different parishes in the former Prussian church provinces beyond the Oder-Neisse border; about 750 records from the Protestant Military Church Registers of the former Prussian army and the German Wehrmacht; and about 70 parish registers from German-speaking congregations outside of Germany. These records can be searched online at **www.ezab.de/kirchenbuecher/kirchenbuch-suche.php.**

You can visit the reading room to consult the records in person if you make a reservation at least two months in advance. Send a letter, fax, or e-mail explaining your subject and purpose of your inquiry (Evangelisches Zentralarchiv, Bethaniendamm 29, 10997 Berlin; fax: 011-49-30-22-50-45-40; e-mail: reservierung@ezab.de). They will let you know whether any of their records are relevant to your research and then ask you to complete an application form.

In the fall of 1944, when it became obvious that the area was in danger of invasion, the church authorities in the various centers—Königsberg (now Kaliningrad), Danzig (Gdańsk), and Stettin (Szczecin)—ordered the ministers of the Evangelical churches to bring all records for shipment to the west in the area of Rhon (near Frankfurt). The great majority of the ministers complied and the books were stored in mine shafts. After the war the Kirchenbücher were damaged by thieves and arsonists, and many were destroyed. No list had been made of the books deposited, so it is not known which were stolen or destroyed and which were retained in the original churches. It is very fortunate that the books from the main centers such as Königsberg (with nineteen parishes) and Stettin (with twenty-two) are virtually complete. There are some records from Danzig but they are by no means complete. A number of the books there were handed over to the church authorities in 1943, but many ministers refused to surrender them when requested. There was a local dispute at the time because some believed the records would be used to discover which inhabitants were Aryan and which were non-Aryan.

At the end of World War II, Paul Langheinrich, a member of the LDS Church, instituted a search for church books and records in the areas occupied by the Soviet forces. He was very successful in this effort and later obtained permission from the Soviet government to take all the books he had found to Berlin. The Red Army even provided a truck for this purpose.

At the same time, the LDS Church entered into negotiations with the Evangelical Church. The LDS officials explained they had no wish to retain the books when they recovered them, but only planned to copy them before returning them to the church. The Evangelical Church agreed to this and fully cooperated with the researchers of the LDS Church. At this time more Kirchenbücher were recovered from the areas I have mentioned and also from areas outside Prussia and Pomerania such as Posen and Silesia.

The Kirchenbücher available for Prussia and Pomerania are too numerous to list in this book, but there is space available to give details of the books from Silesia and Posen. Please bear in mind that the fact that a parish is mentioned does not mean that the records are complete, or that they cover a long period of time, so don't be too excited if you find the name of your ancestral town or village mentioned.

SILESIA (SCHLESIEN): Bunzlau, Goldberg, Grüssau, Hohenfrideberg, Karzem, Königszelt, Leopoldshain, Liegnitz, Marklissa, Reinersdorf, Rothenburg.

POSEN (POZNAŃ): Bromberg, Brostrowe-Friedheim, Cielle, Debenke, Fordon, Gogolin, Grabau, Gross Neudorf, Grünkirch, Krone-an-der-Brahe, Lobsens, Mrotschen, Nakel, Otterau-Langenau, Raschkow, Runowo, Sadke, Schulitz, Schweinert, Schwerin-an-der-Warthe, Sienno, Stenschewo, Weichselhorst, Weissenhöhe, Wilhelmsort, Wirsitz, Wissek, Zduny, Zinsdorf, Zirke.

Some Prussian records were transferred from Merseburg (Sachsen-Anhalt) to Berlin. They include property deeds. Although the records bear the title Secret State Archives Prussian Cultural Heritage (Archivstrasse 12-14 14195 Berlin; phone: 011-49-30-83901-00; e-mail: gsta.pk@ gsta.spk-berlin.de; website: www.gsta.spk-berlin.de/), they are open for genealogical research.

The Federal Archives/Department German Reich (Department R) Berlin Document Center
Bundesarchiv
Finckensteinallee 63
12205 Berlin
Phone: 011-49-30-18-7770-420 Fax: 011-49-30-18-7770-111

E-Mail: berlin@bundesarchiv.de
Website: www.bundesarchiv.de/bundesarchiv/organisation/abteilung_r/
index.html.en

Department R of the Federal Archives contains the records of the
central civil authorities of the German Reich (1867/71–1945), brought
together again after being split apart due to the Second World War and
the division of Germany. Included are the records of the former Berlin
Document Center, which was established after World War II from cap-
tured German files to document the Nazi party and regime from 1920 to
1945. That collection of 30 million documents includes the membership
files of some 10.7 million members of the Nazi Party, as well as personnel files of 600,000 Storm Troopers, 350,000 members of the S.S.,
and 60,000 S.S. officers. All Nazi party officials, SS or SA members,
and government employees had to submit a certified multi-generation
ancestor chart called an *Ahnenpass* to prove Aryan ancestry. You may
find your seventeenth- and eighteenth-century ancestors mentioned in
one of these.

Under the terms of the United States–Germany agreement, all Berlin Document Center records were microfilmed and are available for
public search at the National Archives at College Park (8601 Adelphi
Road, College Park, MD 20740; phone: 301-837-2000; website: www.
archives.gov/research/captured-german-records/foreign-records-seized.
html#center).

**German Center for Genealogy (Deutsche Zentralstelle für
Genealogie)**
Sächsisches Staatsarchiv Leipzig
Schongauer Strasse 1
04329 Leipzig
Phone: 011-49-341-255-5500. Fax: 011-49-341-255-5555
E-mail: poststelle-l@sta.smi.sachsen.de
Website: www.archiv.sachsen.de/6319.htm

The German Center for Genealogy has Germany's largest genealogical
collection and houses many records from the area once known as "East
Germany." Located in the Sachsen (Saxony) State Archives in Leipzig,
it has an extensive collection of church registers, particularly from the
eastern provinces and southeastern Europe; family group sheets; ancestral charts; funeral sermons; local heritage books and card files; and an
assortment of other genealogical collections. The LDS Family History
Library has microfilmed many of the archive's records, including an
extensive collection of German church records, and records of German
settlements in Eastern Europe.

The various holdings include the following:

1. A pedigree and ancestor list that contains more than 12,000 family trees, including over two million card-indexes of individual names. If you are consulting these cards in person (and you may obtain permission to do so), you must know the system. Because of the variation in the spelling of surnames, it was decided to follow a system of phonetic spelling and file under one spelling variation only. So, for example, under the name Maier you will also find Mayer, Meier, and Meyer.

2. A catalogue of personal writings and eulogies. This covers the sixteenth to eighteenth centuries and consists of some 700 works. It is being added to on a regular basis and includes many printed funeral orations and sermons.

3. Photocopies and microfilms of a number of church registers of all denominations.

4. Specialized items, such as a list of the population of Leipzig before 1800, including the surrounding area, and records of the Huguenots who fled from France after the bloody persecution that followed the revocation of the Edict of Nantes in 1685.

5. The library includes 22,000 writings on genealogical subjects, in both published and manuscript form, covering the period from the seventeenth century to the present.

State and Provincial Archives

Landesarchiv Baden-Württemberg
Eugenstrasse 7
70182 Stuttgart
Phone: 011-49-711-212-4272. Fax: 011-49-711-212-4283
E-mail: landesarchiv@la-bw.de
Website: www.landesarchiv-bw.de/

Hauptstaatsarchiv Stuttgart
Konrad-Adenauer-Strasse 4
70173 Stuttgart
Phone: 011-49-711-212-4335. Fax: 011-49-711-212-4360
E-mail: hstastuttgart@la-bw.de
Website: www.landesarchiv-bw.de/web/47272 /

Staatlichen Archive Bayerns
Schönfeldstrasse 5-11
80539 Munich
Phone: 011-49-89-28638-2482. Fax: 011-49-89-28638-2615
E-mail: poststelle@gda.bayern.de
Website: www.gda.bayern.de/

Landesarchiv Berlin
Eichborndamm 115-121
13403 Berlin
Phone: 011-49-30-90264-0. Fax: 011-49-30-90264-201
E-mail: info@landesarchiv.berlin.de
Website: www.landesarchiv-berlin.de/

Brandenburgisches Landeshauptarchiv
Zum Windmühlenberg
(Postfach 600449, 14404 Potsdam)
14469 Potsdam
Phone: 011-49-331-5674-0. Fax: 011-49-331-5674-212
E-mail: poststelle@blha.brandenburg.de
Website: www.landeshauptarchiv-brandenburg.de/

Staatsarchiv Bremen
Am Staatsarchiv 1
28203 Bremen
Phone: 011-49-421-361-6221. Fax: 011-49-421-361-10247
E-mail: office@staatsarchiv.bremen.de
Website: www.staatsarchiv.bremen.de/

Staatsarchiv Hamburg
Kattunbleiche 19
22041 Hamburg
Phone: 011-49-40-428-31-3200. Fax: 011-49-40-428-31-3201
E-mail: poststelle@staatsarchiv.hamburg.de
Website: www.hamburg.de/staatsarchiv

Hessisches Hauptstaatsarchiv
Mosbacher Strasse 55
65187 Wiesbaden
Phone: 011-49-611-881-0. Fax: 011-49-611-881-145
E-mail: poststelle@hhstaw.hessen.de
Website: www.hauptstaatsarchiv.hessen.de/

Landeshauptarchiv Schwerin
Graf-Schack-Alee 2
19053 Schwerin
Phone: 011-49-385-588794-10. Fax: 011-49-385-588794-12
E-mail: poststelle@landeshauptarchiv-schwerin.de
Website: www.kulturwerte-mv.de/

Niedersächsisches Hauptstaatsarchiv
Am Archiv 1
30169 Hannover
Phone: 011-49-511-120-6601. Fax: 011-49-511-120-6699
E-mail: Hannover@nla.niedersachsen.de
Website: www.nla.niedersachsen.de/

Landesarchiv Nordrhein-Westfälisches
Schifferstrasse 30
47059 Duisburg
Phone: 011-49-203-98721-0. Fax: 011-49-203-98721-111
E-mail: poststelle@lav.nrw.de
Website: www.archive.nrw.de/lav/index.php

Landesarchivverwaltung Rheinland-Pfalz
Landeshauptarchiv Koplenz
Karmeliterstrasse 1-3
56068 Koblenz
Phone: 011-49-261-9129-0. Fax: 011-49-261-9129-112
E-mail: post@landeshauptarchiv.de
Website: www.landeshauptarchiv.de/

Landesarchiv Saarbrücken
Dudweilerstrasse 1
66133 Saarbrücken-Scheidt
Phone: 011-49-681-501-00. Fax: 011-49-681-501-1933
E-mail: landesarchiv@landesarchiv.saarland.de
Website: www.saarland.de/landesarchiv.htm

Sächsisches Staatsarchiv
Hauptstaatsarchiv Dresden
Archivstrasse 14
01097 Dresden
Phone: 011-49-351-89219-710. Fax: 011-49-351-89219-709
E-mail: poststelle-d@sta.smi.sachsen.de
Website: www.archiv.sachsen.de/

Landeshauptarchiv Sachsen-Anhalt
Brückstrasse 2
39114 Magdeburg
Phone: 011-49-391-59806-0. Fax: 011-49-391-59806-600
E-mail: poststelle@lha.mi.sachsen-anhalt.de
Website: www.lha.sachsen-anhalt.de/lha/

Landesarchiv Schleswig-Holstein
Prinzenpalais
24837 Schleswig
Phone 011-49-4621-8618-00. Fax: 011-49-4621-8618-01
E-mail: landesarchiv@la.landsh.de
Website: www.landesarchiv.schleswig-holstein.de/

Thüringisches Hauptstaatsarchiv Weimar
Marstallstrasse 2
(Postfach 27 26, 99408 Weimar)
99423 Weimar
Phone: 011-49-36-43-87-198-315. Fax 011-49-36-43-87-198-350
Website: www.thueringen.de/th2/staatsarchive/standorte/weimar/

City Archives (Stadtarchiv)

To locate a particular archive and see what records are available there, try visiting the website **www.archivportal-d.de/**, which allows users to view information on over 400 institutions. The type of record you will find in local archives includes all or some of the following:

Address Books (Adressbücher)
Apprentice Lists (Lehrlingsbücher)
Census Returns (Volkszählungen)
City Chronicles (Stadtchroniken)
City Directories (Adressbücher)
Citizenship Lists (Bürgerbücher)
Court Records (Gerichtsprotokolle)
Emigration Lists (Auswanderungregister)
Family Books (Ortssippenbücher)
Family Registers (Familienregister)
Funeral Sermons (Leichenpredigten)
Grave Registers (Grabregister)
Guild Books (Gilderbücher)
Land Records (Grundbücher)
Lineage Books (Geschlechterbücher)
Newspapers (Zeitungen)
Parish Registers (Kirchenbücher)
Police Registers (Polizeiregister)
Probate Records (Testamente)
Tax Records (Steuerbücher)
Wills (Testamente)

The following abbreviations are used in the list of cities, towns, etc., to show the provinces or Länder in which the places are located:

BW	Baden-Württemberg
B	Bayern
BL	Bremen
BR	Brandenburg
H	Hessen
HL	Hamburg
MV	Mecklenburg-Vorpommern
NS	Niedersachsen
NW	Nordrhein-Westfalen
RP	Rheinland-Pfalz
S	Saarland
SA	Sachsen
SAA	Sachsen-Anhalt
SH	Schleswig-Holstein
T	Thüringen

Aachen (NW)
Aalen (BW)
Abensberg (B)
Ahaus (NW)
Ahrweiler (RP)
Alsfeld (H)
Altdorf (B)
Altena (NW)
Altenburg (SA)
Alt-Wallmoden (NS)
Alzey (RP)
Amlishagen (BW)
Amöneburg (H)
Amstetten (B)
Andernach (RP)
Anklam (MV)
Annaberg-Buckholz
  (SA)
Annweiler (RP)
Ansbach (B)
Apolda (T)
Arnsberg (NW)
Arnstadt (T)
Artern (SAA)
Aschaffenburg (B)
Ascherleben (T)
Aue (SA)
Augsburg (B)
Babenhausen (H)
Bacharach (RP)
Backnang (BW)
Balingen (BW)
Bamberg (B)
Baunatal (H)
Bayreuth (B)
Beeskow (BR)
Bensheim (H)
Bentheim (NS)
Bergisch-Gladbach
  (NW)
Bad Bergzabern (RP)
Berleburg (NW)

Berlin
Bernburg (SAA)
Besighem (BW)
Bevensen (NS)
Biberach (BW)
Bielefeld (NW)
Bingen (RP)
Bischofswerda (SA)
Bitterfeld (SAA)
Blaubeuren (BW)
Blomberg (NW)
Bocholt (NW)
Bochum (NW)
Bonn (NW)
Borken (NW)
Borna (SA)
Bottrop (NW)
Flecken Bovenden
  (NS)
Brafkenheim (BW)
Brakel (NW)
Brandenburg an der
  Havel (BR)
Brandestein bei Elm
  (H)
Braunschweig (NS)
Breckerfeld (NW)
Breisach (BW)
Bremen (BL)
Bremerhaven (BL)
Brilon (NW)
Brühl (NW)
Bad Buchau (BW)
Bühl (BW)
Büren (NW)
Burg auf Fehmarn
  (SH)
Burg bei Magdeburg
  (SAA)
Burgbernheime (B)
Burghausen (B)
Burgkunstadt (B)

Burgsteinfurt (NW)
Burkheim am K
  (BW)
Butzbach (H)
Buxtehude (NS)
Calbe (SAA)
Calw (BW)
Castrop-Rauxel
  (NW)
Celle (NS)
Cham (B)
Chemnitz (SA)
Coburg (B)
Coesfeld (NW)
Coswig (SAA)
Cottbus (BR)
Crimmitschau (SA)
Cuxhaven (NS)
Darmstadt (H)
Deggendorf (B)
Deidesheim (RP)
Delitzch (SA)
Demmin (BR)
Dessau (SAA)
Detmold (NW)
Diez (RP)
Dillingen/Donau (B)
Dingolfing (B)
Dinkelsbühl (B)
Dinslaken (NW)
Doberlug-Kirchhain
  (BR)
Donauwörth (B)
Dornburg/Elbe
  (SAA)
Dorsten (NW)
Dortmund (NW)
Dreieichenhain (H)
Dresden (SA)
Dubeln (SA)
Duderstadt (NS)
Duisburg (NW)

Dulmen (NW)
Düren (NW)
Bad Durkheim (RP)
Düsseldorf (NW)
Eberbach (BW)
Eberswalde (BR)
Ebingen (BW)
Eckernförde (SH)
Edenkoben (RP)
Eggenfelden (B)
Eichstatt (B)
Eilenburg (SA)
Einbeck (NS)
Eisenach (T)
Eisenberg (RP)
Eisenberg (T)
Eisfeld (T)
Eisleben (SAA)
Ellwangen (BW)
Emden (NS)
Emmerich (NW)
Bad Ems (RP)
Endingen (BW)
Engen (BW)
Erding (B)
Erfurt (T)
Erkelenz (NW)
Erlangen (B)
Eschwege (H)
Esslingen/Neckar
 (BW)
Eutin (SH)
Feuchtwangen (B)
Flensburg (SH)
Forchheim (B)
Forst/Lausitz (BR)
Bad Frankenhausen
 (SAA)
Frankenthal (RP)
Frankfurt/Main (H)
Frankfurt/Oder (BR)
Frechen (NW)
Freiberg (SA)

Freiburg/Breisgau
 (BW)
Freising (B)
Freudenstadt (BW)
Friedberg/Hessen (H)
Friedrichshafen
 (BW)
Fritzlar (H)
Fulda (H)
Furstenau (NS)
Furstenwalde (BR)
Fürth (B)
Füssen (B)
Gaildorf (BW)
Gardelegen (SAA)
Garmisch/Parten-
 kirchen (B)
Geinhausen (H)
Geislingen (BW)
Gelsenkirchen (NW)
Gengenbach (BW)
Gera (T)
Gernrode (SAA)
Gerolzhofen (B)
Geseke (NW)
Gevelsberg (NW)
Giengen (BW)
Giessen (H)
Glücksburg (SH)
Glückstadt (SH)
Gnandstein (SA)
Göppingen (BW)
Görlitz (SA)
Goslar (NS)
Gotha (T)
Göttingen (NS)
Greifswald (MV)
Greiz (T)
Greussen (T)
Grimma (SA)
Groitzscg (SA)
Grossbottwar (BW)
Gross-Gerau (B)

Grünberg (H)
Grunstadt (RP)
Guben (BR)
Gudensberg (H)
Güstrow (MV)
Hachenburg (RP)
Hagen (NW)
Halberstadt (SAA)
Halle an der Saale
 (SAA)
Hamburg (HL)
Hameln (NS)
Hanau (H)
Hann/Munden (NS)
Hannover (NS)
Haslach (BW)
Hattingen (NW)
Heidelberg (BW)
Heidenheim/Brenz
 (BW)
Heilbad Heiligen-
 stadt (T)
Helmstedt (NS)
Herberg/Elster (BR)
Herford (NW)
Herne (NW)
Herrenberg (BW)
Hersbruck (B)
Bad Hersfeld (H)
Herten (NW)
Hildburghausen (T)
Hilden (NW)
Hildesheim (NS)
Hochstadt (B)
Hof (B)
Hofgeismar (B)
Homberg (H)
Bad Homberg (H)
Horb/Neckar (BW)
Hornburg (NS)
Höxter (NW)
Hüfingen (BW)
Husum (SH)

Ilmenau (T)
Ingelheim (RP)
Ingoldstadt (B)
Iserlohn (NW)
Isny (BW)
Itzehoe (SH)
Jena (T)
Jever (NS)
Jülich (NW)
Juterbog (BR)
Kaiserlautern (RP)
Kalkar (NW)
Kamenz (SA)
Kandel (RP)
Karlshafen (H)
Karlsruhe (BW)
Karlstadt (B)
Kassel (H)
Kaufbeuren (B)
Kelheim (B)
Kempen (NW)
Kempten/Aligäu (B)
Kenzingen (BW)
Kiel (SH)
Kirchheim/Teck
   (BW)
Kirn (RP)
Kirtorf (H)
Kitzingen (B)
Kleve (NW)
Koblenz (RP)
Köln (NW)
Königshofen (B)
Konstanz (BW)
Korbach/Edersee (H)
Köthen/Anhalt
   (SAA)
Kranenburg (NW)
Krefeld (NW)
Bad Kreuznach (RP)
Kronach (B)
Krönberg (H)
Kulmbach (B)

Kusel (RP)
Lage-Lippe (NW)
Lahnstein (RP)
Lahr (BW)
Landau (RP)
Landsberg (B)
Landshut (B)
Bad Langensalza (T)
Laubach (H)
Lauenburg/Elbe (SH)
Lauf (B)
Laufen (B)
Lauingen/Donau (B)
Lauterbach (H)
Lauterecken (RP)
Leipzig (SA)
Lemgo (NW)
Leutkirch (BW)
Leverkusen (NW)
Lich (H)
Lichtenfels (B)
Limburg/Lahn (H)
Lindau (B)
Linz (RP)
Lippstadt (NW)
Löbau (SA)
Lörrach (BW)
Lubben (BR)
Lübeck (SH)
Luckenwalde (BR)
Lüdenscheid (NW)
Ludwigsburg (BW)
Ludwigshafen (RP)
Ludwigslust (MV)
Lügde (NW)
Lüneburg (NS)
Lünen (NW)
Magdeburg (SAA)
Mainz (RP)
Mannheim (BW)
Marburg (H)
Marienberg (SA)
Markdorf (BW)

Markleeberg (SA)
Marktredwitz (B)
Marl (NW)
Maulbronn (BW)
Mayen (RP)
Meckenheim (NW)
Meersburg (BW)
Meiningen (T)
Meisenheim (RP)
Meissen (SA)
Meldorf (SH)
Melle (NS)
Memmingen (B)
Menden (NW)
Mengen (BW)
Meppen (NS)
Bad Mergentheim
   (BW)
Merseburg (SAA)
Messkirch (BW)
Metelen (NW)
Mettmann (NW)
Meuselwitz (SA)
Michelstadt (H)
Mindelheim (B)
Minden (NW)
Mittweida (SA)
Moers (NW)
Möhringen (BW)
Mönchengladbach
   (NW)
Monschau (NW)
Montabour (RP)
Mühldorf (B)
Mühlhausen/Thur (T)
München (B)
Münnerstadt (B)
Münster (NW)
Bad Münstereifel
   (NW)
Namedy (RP)
Nassau (RP)
Nauheim (H)

Naumburg/Saale (SAA)
Neckarsteinach (H)
Neheim/Hüsten (NW)
Neuburg (B)
Neuenburg (BW)
Neuenhaus (NS)
Neumünster (SH)
Neuötting (B)
Neuss (NW)
Neustadt (B)
Neustadt/Donau (B)
Nidda (H)
Nideggen (NW)
Nordhausen (T)
Nordhorn (NS)
Nordlingen (B)
Northeim (NS)
Nürnberg (B)
Nürtingen (BW)
Oberhausen (NW)
Obernburg/Main (B)
Oberndorf (BW)
Oberursel/Taunas (H)
Oberviechtach (B)
Ochsenfurt (B)
Oelsnitz im Vogtland (SA)
Offenbach/Main (H)
Offenburg (BW)
Ohrdruf (T)
Ohringen (BW)
Oldenburg (SH)
Oldenburg (NS)
Bad Oldesloe (SH)
Olpe (NW)
Opladen (NW)
Oppenheim (RP)
Oranienburg (BR)
Oschatz (SA)
Oschersleben (SAA)
Osnabrück (NS)

Osterburg (SAA)
Osterrode/Harz (NS)
Otterberg (RP)
Otterndorf (NS)
Paderborn (NW)
Paschim (MV)
Pegau (SA)
Perleberg (MV)
Pforzheim (BW)
Pfullendorf (BW)
Pfullingen (BW)
Pirna (SA)
Plauen im Vogtland (SA)
Porz (NW)
Pössneck (T)
Prenzlau (MV)
Pritzwalk (BR)
Bad Pyrmont (NS)
Quakenbrück (NS)
Quedlinnburg (SAA)
Radolfzell (BW)
Rain (B)
Rastatt (BW)
Ratingen (NW)
Ratzeburg (SH)
Ravensburg (BW)
Rees (NW)
Regensburg (B)
Reichenbach im Vogtland (SA)
Reinheim (H)
Remagen (RP)
Remscheid (MW)
Rendsburg (SH)
Reutlingen (BW)
Rheda/Wiedenbrück (NW)
Rheinberg (NW)
Rheine (NW)
Rhein Hausen (NW)
Rheydt (NW)
Rhoden (H)

Riedlingen (BW)
Rieneck (B)
Riesa (SA)
Rinteln (NS)
Rochlitz (SA)
Romrod (H)
Rosberg (NW)
Rosenheim (B)
Rostock (MV)
Rotenburg (NS)
Roth (B)
Rothernburg (B)
Rottweil (BW)
Rudolstadt (T)
Ruhla (T)
Rüthen (NW)
Saalfeld (T)
Saarbrücken (S)
Saarlouis (S)
St. Goar (RP)
St. Ingbert (S)
Salzgitter (NS)
Bad Salzuflen (NW)
Bad Salzungen (T)
Salzwedel (SAA)
Sangerhausen (SAA)
Schalkau (SAA)
Schleiz (T)
Schleswig (SH)
Schleusingen (T)
Schlitz (H)
Schmalkalden (T)
Schmölin (SA)
Schneeberg (SA)
Schönebeck (SAA)
Schongau (B)
Schopfheim (BW)
Schorndorf (BW)
Schotten (H)
Schramberg (BW)
Schwabach (B)
Schwäbisch Gmünd (BW)

Schwäbisch Hall (BW)
Schweinfurt (B)
Schwelm (NW)
Schwerin (MV)
Schwetzingen (BW)
Seefeld (B)
Seehausen/Altmark (SAA)
Seligenstadt (H)
Sendenhorst (NW)
Senftenberg (BR)
Siegburg (NW)
Siegen (NW)
Sigmaringen (BW)
Sindelfingen (BW)
Singen (BW)
Sinsheim (BW)
Sondershausen (T)
Sonneberg (T)
Bad Sooden (H)
Speyer (RP)
Sprendlingen (H)
Stade (NS)
Stadthagen (NS)
Stassfurt (SAA)
Stendal (SAA)
Stockach (BW)
Stockum (NW)
Straelen (NW)
Stralsund (MV)
Straubing (B)
Stuttgart (BW)
Suhl (T)
Sulz/Neckar (BW)
Tangermunde (SAA)
Telgte (NW)

Tittmoning (B)
Bad Tolz (B)
Torgau (SA)
Traunstein (B)
Treffurt (T)
Trier (RP)
Tübingen (BW)
Überlingen (BW)
Uelzen (NS)
Ulm (BW)
Ulrichstein (H)
Unna (NW)
Velbert (NW)
Verden/Aller (NS)
Viersen (NW)
Villingen (BW)
Vohburg/Donau (B)
Volklingen (S)
Wachtenheim (RP)
Waiblingen (BW)
Bad Waldsee (BW)
Waldheim (SA)
Waldshut (BW)
Wangen (BW)
Wanne-Eickel (NW)
Warendorf (NW)
Warstein (NW)
Wasserburg am Inn (B)
Wattenscheid (NW)
Weiden-Oberpfalz (B)
Weil am Rhein (BW)
Weilburg (H)
Weilheim (B)
Weimar (T)
Weingarten (BW)

Weinheim (BW)
Weismain (B)
Weissenburg (B)
Weissenfels (SAA)
Werl (NW)
Werne an der Lippe (NW)
Wernigerode (SAA)
Wertheim (BW)
Wesel (NW)
Wetzlar (H)
Wiesbaden (H)
Wilster (SH)
Bad Wimpfen (BW)
Bad Windsheim (B)
Winsen (S)
Wismar (MV)
Witten (NW)
Wolfach (BW)
Wolfenbüttel (NS)
Wolgast (MV)
Wolmirstedt (SAA)
Wormeln (NW)
Worms (RP)
Wülfrath (NW)
Wünsiedel (B)
Wuppertal (NW)
Würzburg (B)
Xanten (NW)
Zeitz (SAA)
Zella-Mehlis (T)
Zerbst (SAA)
Zeulenroda (T)
Zittau (SA)
Zweibrücken (RP)
Zwickau (SA)

I do not claim that the above list is complete. It has been put together from a variety of sources, and there will be omissions, particularly of smaller places. Any "snail mail" correspondence should be sent to the Direktor, Stadtarchiv, followed by the name of the city and the province or Länder.

In addition to the above, there are specialized archives in such places as Jena, for example, where you will find the archives of the Carl Zeiss Company (**www.zeiss.com/corporate/en_de/history/archives.html**) and the former Jena Glassworks (now Schott). If you know your ancestor worked for a large corporation, it may be worthwhile to contact the company concerned to ask if it has archival or personnel records available.

Parish Archives (Pfarrarchiv)

Many of the city archives shown above also have local church records, but there are also separate church archives. See Chapter 5 for a list of parishes with archives holding Catholic and/or Lutheran records.

Family Archives (Familienarchiv)

Many of the princely, noble, or prominent German families have either donated their family papers and records to the state or opened their documents to the general public. Searches can be made without charge, or by a fee, according to local decision. These family archives may be located in the original family residence (usually a Schloss, or castle) or in archives in the state, city, or village. If your ancestors were employed by these families, or were tenant farmers on the estate, the information can be of very great value to you.

The family archives I have been able to discover are listed below, showing the place, the abbreviation for the province or Länder, and the name of the family. (*Note*: The province codes are the same as those used above.)

Adelebsen (NS), Adelebsen
Ahausen (NW), Spee
Alme (NW), Spee zu Alme
Altenhof (SH), Reventlow
Althausen (BW), Württemberg
Amecke (NW), Wrede-Amecke
Amorbach (B), Leiningen
Anholt (NW), Salm
Antfeld (NW), Papen zu Antfeld
Apelern (NS), Münchhausen
Artelshofen (B), Harlach
Aschhausen (BW), Zeppelin
Assenheim (H), Solms-
    Rödelheim
Assumstadt (BW), Waldburg-
    Wolfegg
Aufsess (B), Aufsess

Augsburg (B), Fugger
Aulendorf (BW), Königsegg-
    Aulendorf
Banteln (NS), Benningsen
Beetzendorf (SAA), Von der
    Schulenburg
Beichlingen (T), Werthern-
    Beichlingen
Bentlage (NW), Wittgenstein-
    Berleburg
Berleburg (NW), Wittgenstein-
    Berleburg
Besselich (RP), Barton-Stedman
Bietigheim (BW), Hornstein
Binningen (BW), Hornstein
Birkenau (H), Unstadt
Birstein (H), Isenburg

Bödigheim (BW), Collenberg
Bodman (BW), Bodman
Boltzenburg (MV), Von Arnim
Haus Borg (NW), Kerkerinck
Braunfels (H), Solms-Braunfels
Breitenburg (SH), Rantzau
Breitenhaupt (NW), Kanne
Haus Brinke (NW), Korff-Bilkau
Buchholz (BW), Ow
Budingen (H), Ysenburg
Buldern (NW), Romberg
Burgsteinfurt (NW), Bentheim
Burkeim (BW), Fahnenberg
Caen (NW), Geyr
Calmsweiler (S), Buseck-Weber
Canstein (NW), Elverfeldt
Cappenberg (NW), Stein
Castell (B), Castell
Celle (NS), Lüneberg
Coesfeld (NW), Salm-Horstmar
Corvey (NW), Ratibor
Crassenstein (NW), Ansembourg
Crollage (NW), Ledebur
Dalwigksthal (H), Dalwigk
Darfeld (NW), Vischering
Derneburg (NS), Münster
Deutsch-Nienhof (SH),
    Hedemann-Heespen
Die Poltsdorf (B), Enderndorf
Diersburg (BW), Roeder
Diersfordt (NW), Wernigerode
Dillingen (B), Fuggers
Donaueschingen (BW),
    Fürstenberg
Donzdorf (BW), Rechberg
Drensteinfurt (NW), Landsberg-
    Velen
Dresden (SA), Wolkenstein
Bad Driburg (NW), Oeynhausen
Dulmen (NW), Croy
Durbach (BW), Windschläg
Dyck (NW), Reifferscheidt
Ebnet (BW), Gayling

Egelborg (NW), Oer
Eglofs (BW), Syrgenstein
Eichtersheim (BW), Venning
Elbenberg (H), Buttlar
Ellingen (B), Wrede
Eltville (H), Eltz
Erbach (H), Erbach
Erpernberg (NW), Wartenberg-
    Brenken
Erzeleben (SAA), Alvensleben
Eschenbach (B), Eschenbach
Essingen (BW), Woellwarth
Eybach (BW), Degenfeld-
    Schonburg
Fachsenfeld (BW), Fachsenfeld
Fischbach (B), Enderndorf
Frankenberg (B), Pöllnitz
Frankisch-Crumbach (H),
    Gemmingen
Furth-Burgfarrnbach (B), Pückler
Gärtringen (BW), Gärtringen
Gemünd (NW), Harff-Dreiborn
Gemünden (RP), Salis-Soglio
Gersfeld (H), Ebersberg-Froberg
Gödens (NS), Wedel
Göppingen (BW), Liebenstein
Gotha (T), Hohenlohe
Greifenberg (B), Perfall
Grevenburg (NW), Oeynhausen
Gross-Brunsrode (NS), Bülow
Grünsberg (B), Reichenbach
Guttenberg (B), Guttenberg
Burg-Guttenberg (BW),
    Gemmingen
Hahnstatten (RP), Bieberstein
Haidenburg (B), Aretin
Haimendorf (B), Rehlingen
Harff (NW), Mirbach
Havixbeck (NW), Twikkel
Heimerzheim (NW), Böselager
Heltorf (NW), Spee
Herbern (NW), Merveldt
Herdringen (NW), Fürstenberg

Heroldsberg (B), Geuder
Herrnstein (NW), Reichenstein
Hinnenburg (NW), Asseburg
Hohenstadt (BW), Adelmann
Höllinghofen (NW), Böselager
Hornberg (BW), Gemmingen
Hugstetten (BW), Mentzingen
Irmelshausen (B), Bibra
Jagsthausen (BW), Berlichingen
Jettingen-Eberstall (B),
    Stauffenberg
Kalbeck (NW), Vittinghoff
Kellenberg (NW), Hoensbroech
Kendenich (NW), Kempis
Kleinbottwar (BW), Schaubek
Königseggwald (BW), Aulendorf
Korschenbroich (NW),
    Wüllenweber
Kronburg (B), Westernach
Laibach (BW), Racknitz
Langenstein (BW), Douglas
Laubach (H), Solms-Laubach
Lauterbach (H), Riedesel
Lenthe (NS), Lenthe
Lich (H), Solms-Lich
Lipporg (NW), Galen
Loburg (NW), Elverfeldt
Marck (NW), Grüter
Marxwalde (BR), Hardenberg
Massenbach (BW), Massenbach
Merkstein (NW), Brauchitsch
Merlsheim (NW), Mühlen
Mespelbrunn (B), Ingelheim
Meuselwitz (SA), Seckendorff
Mitwitz (B), Würtzburg
Moyland (NW), Steengracht
Nassau (RP), Stein
Neuenburg (B), Gagern
Neuenstein (BW), Hohenlohe
Neunhof (B), Welser
Neuwied (RP), Wied
Niedenstein (BW), Venning

Niederstotzingen (BW),
    Maldegem
Oberbalzheim (BW), Balzheim
Obernzenn (B), Seckendorff
Oberstadion (BW), Schönborn
Öhringen (BW), Hohenlohe
Ostwig (NW), Lüninck
Ottingen (B), Ottingen
Pöttmes (B), Gumppenberg
Rammersdorf (B), Eyb
Ratzenried (BW), Trauchberg
Regensburg (B), Thurn-Taxis
Rentweinsdorf (B), Rotenhan
Rheda-Wiedenbrück (NW),
    Tecklenburg
Rösberg (NW), Weichs
Rötha (SA), Friesen
Rugland (B), Crailsheim
Ruhr (NW), Mühlen
Rust (BW), Böcklinsau
Schatthausen (BW), Ravensburg
Schillingsfürst (B), Hohenlohe
Schlatt (BW), Reischach
Schlitz (H), Görtz
Schönstein (RP), Wildenburg
Schopfheim (BW), Roggenbach
Schwarmstedt (NS), Lenthe
Schwarzenberg (B), Schwarzen-
    berg
Schwarzenraben (NW), Ketteler
Schweinsberg (H), Schweinsberg
Sigmaringen (BW), Hohenzollern
Simmelsdorf (B), Simmelsdorf
Singen (BW), Enzenberg
Somborn (H), Savigny
Stapel (NW), Raitz-Frentz-Droste
Steisslingen (BW), Stotzingen
Stetten (BW), Stetten
Sulzfeld (BW), Ravensburg
Surenberg (NW), Heereman-
    Zuydtwyck
Syburg (B), Geyern

Tambach (B), Ortenburg
Tannhausen (BW), Thannhausen
Tannheim (BW), Schaesberg
Thurnau (B), Giech
Trier (RP), Kesselstatt
Trockau (B), Trockau
Ullstadt (B), Frankenstein
Volkershausen (B), Stein-
 Ostheim
Vörden (NW), Haxthausen
Vornholz (NW), Nagel-Doornick
Waake (NS), Wangenheim
Waal (B), Leyen
Wachendorf (BW), Ow-
 Wachendorf
Wallerstein (B), Oettingen
Warthausen (BW), Warthausen

Weeze (NW), Loë
Weissenburg (B), Geyern
Welbergen (NW), Welbergen
Wernstein (B), Künsberg
Wertheim (BW), Löwenstein-
 Wertheim
Westerholt (NW), Westerholt
Westerwinkel (NW), Merveldt
Wewer (NW), Brenken
Wiesentheid (B), Wiesentheid
Wittgenstein (NW), Wittgenstein-
 Hohenstein
Wolfegg (BW), Waldburg-
 Wolfegg
Worms (RP), Hernsheim
Zeil (BW), Waldburg-Zeil

Libraries (Bibliotheken)

The public libraries in cities and towns should not be neglected as a source of information. They usually contain city directories, newspapers, and local histories, all of which may date back to the middle or early part of the nineteenth century. In many places names have been abstracted from early newspapers and placed on index cards. Many libraries also contain details of local families if they have taken an active part in the affairs of the district.

Chapter 9:
Genealogical
Associations in Germany

There are a number of genealogical associations in Germany. Many are members of a national genealogical association: Deutsche Arbeitsgemeinschaft genealogischer Verbände e.V., known as the DAGV (c/o Dirk Weissleder, Vorsitzender, Ginsterweg 12, 30880 Laatzen; e-mail: info@dagv.org; website: www.dagv.org/). Below is a list of most of the DAGV member associations. It is important that you make contact with the one operating in your area of Germany because (a) they will probably know if someone else has already researched your family; (b) many of them have their own libraries and archives, which may contain items of vital interest to you; (c) many of them publish magazines at regular intervals and will publish small ads or queries, either free or for a small charge. Some of them only accept queries for their own members, so you might consider joining.

The DAGV does not perform any research itself, but if you send an inquiry to them, they will give you advice in English, or at least let you know where to direct your inquiries. Your request should contain as many details as possible about the person you are researching, including family name, first name(s), dates and places of birth or baptism, marriage or divorce, and death or burial. The DAGV doesn't charge for its service; however, donations are welcome.

Bear in mind that addresses can change, and there can always be additions or deletions. Check the DAGV website for the most up-to-date contact information for their member associations.

Regional Societies
Werkgroep Genealogisch Onderzoek Duitsland (WGOD)
c/o J. J. Kaldenbach

Amstelstraat 18
NL-1823 EV **Alkmaar, Niederlande**
E-mail: voorzitter-wgod@wgod.nl
Website: www.wgod.nl

Upstalsboom-Gesellschaft für historische Personenforschung und
Bevölkerungsgeschichte in Ostfriesland e.V.
Fischteichweg 16
26603 **Aurich**
E-mail: upstalsboom-gesellschaft@t-online.de
Website: www.upstalsboom.org

Institut für Personengeschichte
Hauptstrasse 65
64625 **Bensheim**
E-mail: v.lehsten@personengeschichte.de
Website: www.personengeschichte.de

Arbeitsgemeinschaft für Familiengeschichte im Kulturkreis Siemens e.V.
13623 **Berlin**

HEROLD Verein für Heraldik, Genealogie und verwandte Wissen-
schaften
Archivstrasse 11
14195 **Berlin-Dahlem**
E-Mail: geschaeftsstelle@herold-verein.de
Website: www.herold-verein.de/

Gruppen Familien- und Wappenkunde in der Stiftung Bahn-Sozialwerk
(GFW/BSW)
Rauks Feld 5A
44869 **Bochum**
E-mail: herbert.kuba@gmx.de
Website: http://gfw.genealogy.net

Arbeitsgemeinschaft Genealogie Braunschweig e.V.
Forststrasse 46A
38108 **Braunschweig**
Website: http://genealogen-in-braunschweig.genealogy.net/

Die Maus, Gesellschaft für Familienforschung e.V. (Bremen)
Am Staatsarchiv 1/Fedelhören
28203 **Bremen**
E-mail: archiv@die-maus-bremen.de
Website: www.die-maus-bremen.de

Familienkundliche Arbeitsgemeinschaft der Männer vom Morgenstern,
Heimatbund an Elb- und Wesermündung e.V.
Burgstrasse 1
27570 **Bremerhaven**

E-mail: vorstand@m-v-m.de
Website: www.m-v-m.de

Schadow-Gesellschaft e.V.
Am Wassertrum 11
29223 **Celle**
E-mail: info@schadow-gesellschaft.org
Website: www.schadow-gesellschaft.org/

Verein für Familienforschung in Ost- und Westpreussen e.V. (VFFOW)
Reinhard Wenzel
An der Leegde 23
29223 **Celle**
E-mail: hardiwenzel@t-online.de
Website: www.vffow.de

Genealogischer Verein Chemnitz e.V.
Postfach 71 01 54
09056 **Chemnitz**
E-mail: genchemnitz@gmx.de
Website: www.gv-chemnitz.de/

Hessische familiengeschichtliche Vereinigung e.V.
Karolinenplatz 3 (Staatsarchiv)
64289 **Darmstadt**
E-mail: hfv@haus-der-geschichte.com
Website: www.hfv-ev.de/

Familienstiftung Pies-Archiv, Forschungszentrum Vorderhunsrück e.V.
Altes Pfarrhaus
An der Kirche 1
56290 **Dommershausen**
E-mail: info@familienstiftungpies-archiv-museum.de
Website: www.familienstiftungpies-archiv-museum.de/

Roland zu Dortmund e.V.
Genealogisch-heraldische Arbeitsgemeinschaft
Postfach 103341
44033 **Dortmund**
E-mail: info@roland-zu-dortmund.de

Dresdner Verein für Genealogie e.V.
PF 19 25 03
01283 **Dresden**
E-mail: kontakt@dresden-genealogieverein.de
Website: www.dresden-genealogieverein.de/

Landesarchiv Nordrhein-Westfalen Abteilung Rheinland Standort Brühl
Schifferstrasse 30
47059 **Duisburg**

E-mail: rheinland@lav.nrw.de
Website: www.archive.nrw.de

Historischer Verein Wolhynien e.V.
c/o Gerhard König, Neustadt 14
99817 **Eisenach**
E-mail: hivewo@wolhynien.de
Website: http://historischerverein.wolhynien.de

Vereinigung für Familienkunde Elmshorn
Beate Claßen, Bi de Möhl 10 b
25336 **Elmshorn**
E-mail: beaclas@yahoo.de
Website: www.elmshorn.de/

Arbeitsgemeinschaft Genealogie Thüringen e.V. (AGT)
Verein für Heimat-, Familien- und Wappenkunde
Herderstrasse 35
99096 **Erfurt**
E-mail: pjklipp@online.de
Website: www.genealogie-thueringen.de

Genealogischer Kreis Siemens Erlangen
c/o Freizeitgemeinschaft Siemens Erlangen e.V
Hartmannstrasse 17
91052 **Erlangen**
Website: http://gksiemens.genealogy.net

Zentralstelle für Personen- und Familiengeschichte (Institut für
Genealogie)
c/o Peter Dümig
Brauhannsweg 42a
61381 **Friedrichsdorf**
E-mail: peter.duemig@genealogische-zentralstelle.de
Website: www.genealogie-institut.de/

Arbeitskreis Familien- und Ahnenforschung Geislingen/steige e.V.
Bühlstrasse 41
89547 **Gerstetten-Gussenstadt**
E-mail: vorsitzender(a)afagev.de
Website: http://afagev.de/

Genealogische Gesellschaft Goslar
c/o Ulrich Albers
Stadtarchiv Goslar
Zehntstrasse 24
38640 **Goslar**

Genealogisch-Heraldische Gesellschaft Göttingen e.V.
Postfach 2062
37010 **Göttingen**

E-mail: ghgg@genealogy.net
Website: http://ghgg.genealogy.net/

Arbeitskreis für Siebenbürgische Landeskunde e.V. (AKSL)
Sektion Genealogie
Schloss Horneck
74831 **Gundelsheim/Neckar**
E-mail: institut@sb-gun1.bib-bw.de
Website: http://siebenbuergen-institut.de/familienforschung

Arbeitskreis für Familienforschung im Hagener Heimatbund e.V.
Eilper Strasse 71
58091 **Hagen**
E-mail: info@hagenerheimatbund.de
Website: www.hagenerheimatbund.de

Genealogische Gesellschaft Hamburg e.V.
Postfach 302042
20307 **Hamburg**
E-mail: info@FFHHeV.de
Website: www.GGHHeV.de/

Verband deutschsprachiger Berufsgenealogen e.V.
Cheruskerweg 1
22525 **Hamburg**
E-mail: info@berufsgenealogie.net
Website: www.berufsgenealogie.net

Niedersächsischer Landesverein für Familienkunde e.V. (NLF)
Rückertstraße 1
30169 **Hannover**
E-mail: info@familienkunde-niedersachsen.de
Website: www.familienkunde-niedersachsen.de

Heraldischer Verein Zum Kleeblatt von 1888 zu Hannover e.V.
Spandauer Weg 59
31141 **Hildesheim**
E-mail: info@zum-kleeblatt.de
Website: www.zum-kleeblatt.de/

Pommerschen Greif e.V., Verein für Familien- und Ortsgeschichts-
forschung
Neue Strasse 19
21702 **Kakerbeck**
Website: www.pommerscher-greif.de/

Gesellschaft für Familienkunde in Kurhessen und Waldeck e.V. (GFKW)
Postfach 10 13 46
34013 **Kassel**
E-mail: info@gfkw.de
Website: www.gfkw.de/

Arbeitsgemeinschaft für mitteldeutsche Familienforschung e.V. (AMF)
Neue Sorge 77
06537 **Kelbra**
E-mail: vorstand@amf-verein.de
Website: www.amf-verein.de

Oldenburgische Gesellschaft für Familienkunde e.V.
Marktplatz 6
26209 **Kirchhatten**
E-mail: ogf@familienkunde-oldenburg.de
Website: www.familienkunde-oldenburg.de

Leps-Mielke Stiftung
c/o Dr.-Ing. Harald Howe
Cohnenhofstrasse 96d
50769 **Köln-Langel-Cohnenhof**
E-Mail: dr.howe@netcologne.de

Leipziger Genealogische Gesellschaft e.V.
Martina Wermes
c/o Sächsisches Staatsarchiv, Staatsarchiv Leipzig
Schongauerstrasse 1
04328 **Leipzig**
E-Mail: info@lgg-leipzig.de
Internet: www.lgg-leipzig.de

Verein für Familienforschung e.V. Lübeck
Mühlentorplatz 2 (Mühlentorturm)
23552 **Lübeck**
Website: http://familienforschung-luebeck.de/

Pfälzisch-Rheinische Familienkunde e.V.
Rottstrasse 17
67061 **Ludwigshafen**
E-mail: prfk-lu@gmx.de
Website: www.prfk.org/

Verein für Computergenealogie e.V.
Schorlemmers Kamp 20
44536 **Luenen**
E-mail: compgen@genealogy.net
Website: http://compgen.genealogy.net

Interessengemeinschaft Ahnenforscher Ländle (IGAL)
Morgenstrasse 13
A-6890 **Lustenau**
E-mail: info@igal.at
Website: www.igal.at/

Arbeitsgemeinschaft Genealogie Magdeburg
Thiemstrasse 7 (Literaturhaus)
39104 **Magdeburg**
E-Mail: agmagdeburg@genealogienetz.de
Website: www.genealogienetz.de/vereine/AG-Magdeburg/

Arbeitskreis Familienforschung der Emsländischen Landschaft e.V.
Am Neuen Markt 1
49716 **Meppen/Ems**
E-mail: info@ genealogie-emsland-bentheim.de
Website: www.genealogie-emsland-bentheim.de/

Bayerischer Landesverein für Familienkunde e.V.
Metzstrasse 14b
81667 **München**
E-Mail: blf@blf-online.de
Website: www.blf-online.de/

Münchner Wappen Herold e.V.
Pariser Strasse 8
81669 **München**
E-mail: info@muenchner-wappen-herold.de
Website: www.muenchner-wappen-herold.de/

Bund der Familienverbände e.V. (BdF)
Bundesgeschäftsstelle
Rektoratsweg 123/25
48159 **Münster**
E-mail: info@bund-der-familienverbaende.de
Website: www.bund-der-familienverbaende.de

Stiftung Stoye
c/o Steffen Iffland, Vorstand
Bochumner Strasse 157
99734 **Nordhausen**
E-mail: vorstand@stiftung-stoye.org
Website: www.stiftung-stoye.org

Gesellschaft für Familienforschung in Franken e.V. (GFF)
Vordere Cramergasse 13
90478 **Nürnberg**
E-mail: info@gf-franken.de
Website: www.gf-franken.de/

Arbeitskreis Familienforschung Osnabrück e.V.
c/o Landhaus Mehring
Iburger Strasse 240
49082 **Osnabrück**
E-mail: post@osfa.de
Website: www.osfa.de

Arbeitsgemeinschaft ostdeutscher Familienforscher e.V. (AGoFF)
Mario Seifert
Hessestrasse 16
14469 **Potsdam**
E-mail: kontakt@agoff.de
Website: www.agoff.de/

Brandenburgische Genealogische Gesellschaft - Roter Adler e.V.
Postfach 60 05 18
14405 **Potsdam**
E-mail: vs@bggroteradler.de
Website: www.bggroteradler.de/

Arbeitsgemeinschaft für Saarländische Familienkunde e.V. (ASF)
Geschäftsstelle: Norbert Emanuel
Hebbelstrasse 3
66346 **Püttlingen**
E-mail: asf.ev@online.de
Website: www.asf-saargenealogie.de

Düsseldorfer Verein für Familienkunde e.V.
Krummenweger Strasse 26
40885 **Ratingen-Lintorf**
E-mail: dvff582@arcor.de
Website: www.dvff.de

Vereinigung Sudetendeutscher Familienforscher e.V. (VSFF)
Landshuter Strasse 4
93047 **Regensburg**
E-mail: vorsitzender@vsff.de
Website: www.sudetendeutsche-familienforscher.de/

Schleswig-Holsteinische Familienforschung e.V. (SHFam)
c/o Landesarchiv Schleswig-Holstein
Prinzenpalais
24837 **Schleswig**
E-mail: shfam@genealogy.net
Website: http://shfam.genealogy.net

Verein für Genealogie in Nordwürttemberg e.V
Auf dem Katzenkopf 34
74523 **Schwäbisch Hall**
E-mail: vorstand2008@ahnenforscher-heilbronn.de
Website: www.genealogie-nordwuerttemberg.de

Arbeitskreis donauschwäbischer Familienforscher (AKdFF) e.V.
Goldmühlestrasse 30
71065 **Sindelfingen**
E-mail: info@akdff.de
Website: http://akdff.de

Verein für Familien- und Wappenkunde in Württemberg und Baden e.V.
Postfach 105441
70047 **Stuttgart**
E-mail: wappen@wlb-stuttgart.de
Website: www.vfwkwb.org

Gesellschaft für Familienforschung in der Oberpfalz e.V.
c/o Dr. Volker Wappmann
Friedrichstrasse 16
92648 **Vohenstrauss**
E-mail: volker_wappmann@web.de
Website: http://gfo.genealogy.net

Verein für Mecklenburgische Familien- und Personengeschichte e.V.
(MFP)
Andreas Parlow, c/o Thünen-Museum-Tellow
OT Tellow
17168 **Warnkenhagen**
E-mail: Vorstand@MFPeV.de
Website: www.mfpev.de/

Familienkundliche Gesellschaft für Nassau und Frankfurt e.V.
Mosbacher Strasse 55 (Hessisches Hauptstaatsarchiv)
65187 **Wiesbaden**
E-mail: familienkunde.nassau@email.de
Website: http://fgnff.genealogy.net

Bergischer Verein für Familienkunde e.V. (BVfF e.V.)
c/o Hans-Friedrich Kartenbender
Hausfeld 38
42339 **Wuppertal**
E-mail: vorstand@bvff.de
Website: www.bvff.de

There are also some organizations concerned with more specific
subjects:

Anglo-German FHS, Mrs Gwen Davis, BA (Hons), 5 Oldbury Grove,
Beaconsfield, Buckinghamshire, England, United Kingdom, HP9 2AJ;
e-mail: gwedolinedavis@aol.com; website: www.agfhs.org/

Mennonitischer Geschichtsverein, Am Hollerbrunnen 2A, 67295 Bo-
landen Weierhof; website: www.mennoniten.de/geschichtsverein.html

Salzburger Verein e. V., Memeler Strasse 35, 33605 Bielefeld; e-mail:
info@salzburgerverein.de; website: http://salzburgerverein.de/

The following organizations are sources of information about **Huguenotten (Huguenots)**:

Deutsche Hugenotten-Gesellschaft e.V. (DHG), Deutsches Hugenotten-Zentrum, Hafenplatz 9a, 34385 Bad Karlshafen; e-mail: info@hugenotten.de; website: www.hugenotten.de/

Consistorium der Französischen Kirche, Joachim-Friedrich-Strasse 4, 10711 Berlin; e-mail: buero@franzoesische-kirche.de; website: www.franzoesische-kirche.de/

There are also hundreds of historical associations and societies in all the major cities and towns. It is impossible to list them all, but a search on the Internet should produce results. Historical organizations very often have a great deal of information about local families even if genealogy is not the main object of their existence.

CHAPTER 10:
GERMAN GENEALOGICAL
ASSOCIATIONS IN NORTH
AMERICA

Included here is a list of some of the German genealogical societies in North America. You can search on the Internet to see if there are any other societies in your area. I hope readers will realize that in many voluntary organizations addresses change with the change of officials, so you should check the society's website for the most current contact information.

THE UNITED STATES

American Historical Society of Germans from Russia
631 D Street, Lincoln, NE 68502-1199
Phone: 402-474-3363. Fax: 402-474-7229
E-mail: ahsgr@ahsgr.org
Website: www.ahsgr.org/

American/Schleswig-Holstein Heritage Society
PO Box 506, Walcott, IA 52773-0506
Phone: 563-284-4184. Fax: 563-284-4184
E-mail: ashhs@ashhs.org
Website: www.ashhs.org/

Berks County Genealogical Society
201 Washington Street
Reading, PA 19601
Phone: 610-921-4970
E-mail: berksgenes@dejazzd.com
Website: www.berksgenes.org/

The Danube Swabian Association of Trenton, New Jersey
127 Route 156
Yardville, NJ 08620
Phone: 609-585-1932
E-mail: dsa@trentondonauschwaben.com
Website: www.trentondonauschwaben.com

Donauschwaben Heritage Society
E-mail: info@banaters.com
Website: www.banaters.com

Genealogical Society of Pennsylvania
2207 Chestnut Street, Philadelphia, PA 19103
Phone: 215-545-0391
E-mail: ExecDir@genpa.org
Website: www.genpa.org/

German-Acadian Coast Historical & Genealogical Society
PO Box 3086
LaPlace, Louisiana 70069-3086
Website: www.gachgs.com

German-Bohemian Heritage Society
PO Box 822
New Ulm, MN 56073-0822
Website: www.rootsweb.ancestry.com/~gbhs/

The German Society of Pennsylvania
611 Spring Garden Street
Philadelphia, PA 19123
Phone: 215-627-2332. Fax: 215-627-5297
E-mail: info@germansociety.org
Website: www.germansociety.org

German-Texan Heritage Society
PO Box 684171
Austin, TX 78768-4171
Phone: 512-467-4569. Fax: 512-467-4574
E-mail: info@germantexans.org
Website: www.germantexans.org

Germanic Genealogy Society
PO Box 16312
St. Paul, MN 55116-0312
E-mail: info@ggsmn.org
Website: www.ggsmn.org/

Germans from Russia Heritage Society
1125 West Turnpike Avenue
Bismarck, ND 58501
Phone: 701-223-6167. Fax: 701-223-4421

E-mail: rachel@grhs.org
Website: www.grhs.org/

Illinois Mennonite Historical & Genealogical Society
675 State Route 116
Metamora, IL 61548-7732
Phone: 309-367-2551
E-mail: imhc@mtco.com
Website: www.imhgs.org

Immigrant Genealogical Society
PO Box 7369
Burbank, CA 91510-7369
Phone: 818-848-3122. Fax: 818-716-6300
Website: www.immigrantgensoc.org/

Lancaster Mennonite Historical Society
2215 Millstream Road
Lancaster, PA 17602-1499
Phone: 717-393-9745. Fax: 717-393-8751
E-mail: lmhs@lmhs.org
Website: www.lmhs.org/

Mennonite Heritage Center
565 Yoder Road
Harleysville, PA 19438-1020
Phone: 215-256-3020
E-mail: info@mhep.org
Website: www.mhep.org/

Mid-Atlantic Germanic Society
Membership: c/o Gunter Schanzenbacher
725 Fir Spring Drive
Waynesboro, PA 17268-2914
E-mail: Membership@magsgen.com
Website: www.magsgen.com/

Orangeburgh German-Swiss Genealogical Society
PO Box 974
Orangeburg, SC 29116-0974
Website: www.ogsgs.org/

Ostfriesen Genealogical Society of America
1670 South Robert Street, #333
West St. Paul, MN 55118
E-mail: info@ogsa.us
Website: www.ogsa.us/

Palatines to America
PO Box 141260
Columbus, OH 43214

Phone: 614-267-4700
E-mail: membership@palam.org
Website: www.palam.org/
(There are state chapters in Colorado, Illinois, Indiana, New York, North Carolina, Ohio, and Pennsylvania.)

The Pennsylvania German Society
PO Box 118
Ephrata, PA 17522
Phone: 717-597-7940
E-mail: pgs@innernet.net
Website: www.pgs.org/

Pommerscher Verein Freistadt
PO Box 204
Germantown, WI 53022-0204
E-mail: information@pommerschervereinfreistadt.org
Website: http://pommerschervereinfreistadt.org/

Polish Genealogical Society of America
984 N. Milwaukee Avenue
Chicago, IL 60642-4101
E-mail: PGSAmerica@pgsa.org
Website: www.pgsa.org/

Sacramento German Genealogy Society
PO Box 660061
Sacramento, CA 95866-0061
Phone: 916-361-2956
E-mail: sggs@sggs.us
Website: www.sacgergensoc.org/

Schwenkfelder Library and Heritage Center
105 Seminary Street
Pennsburg, PA 18073
Phone: 215-679-3103. Fax: 215-679-8175
E-mail: info@schwenkfelder.com
Website: www.schwenkfelder.com/

South Central Pennsylvania Genealogical Society
PO Box 1824
York, PA 17405-1824
E-mail: scpgswebsite@wildblue.net
Website: http://scpgs.org/

CANADA

East European Genealogical Society
PO Box 2536
Winnipeg, Manitoba R3C 4A7
Phone: 204-989-3292
E-mail: info@eegsociety.org
Website: www.eegsociety.org/

Society for German Genealogy in Eastern Europe
Box 905 Stn. M
Calgary, Alberta T2P 2J6
E-mail: membership@sggee.org
Website: www.sggee.org/

Waterloo Region Branch, Ontario Genealogical Society
Kitchener Public Library (Grace Schmidt Room)
85 Queen Street North
Kitchener, Ontario N2H 2H1
E-mail: watogs@yahoo.com
Website: www.waterlooogs.ca/

CHAPTER 11:
ONLINE RESOURCES

Below are some websites that provide searchable databases, digitized images of records, or other helpful information for researchers. You will also find numerous other websites listed throughout this book that will be invaluable in your online family history research.

General Resources and Portals

www.ancestry.com
Baden, Brandenburg, and Wuerttemberg emigration lists, city directories, and more.

www.archivportal-d.de
Enables users to comb through Germany's archives free of charge.

www.archivportal.niedersachsen.de/
Archive portal for Lower Saxony.

www.archiv.sachsen.de/6319.htm
Germany's largest genealogical collection.

www.cyndislist.com/germany.htm
German research links in all kinds of categories.

www.rootsweb.ancestry.com/~romban/misc/germanjobs.html
German to English list of old German professions.

https://familysearch.org
Numerous German church and vital records.

www.genealogienetz.de/genealogy.html
An English-language portal to German genealogy databases and services.

www.ortsfamilienbuecher.de/
Lists of heritage books (which list all residents of a village with births, marriages, and deaths for a specific time period) published online.

www.rootsweb.ancestry.com/~wggerman
Germany GenWeb Project.

Handwriting and Letter-Writing Guides
https://familysearch.org/learn/wiki/en/Germany_Handwriting
Old German handwriting tools and examples.

**https://familysearch.org/learn/wiki/en/Germany_Letter_Writing_
Guide**
German letter-writing guide.

http://feefhs.org/guides/German_Gothic.pdf
Handwriting guide for German Gothic.

https://script.byu.edu/Pages/German/en/welcome.aspx
German script tutorial.

Immigration
http://aad.archives.gov/aad/series-list.jsp?cat=GP44
Data files relating to the immigration of Germans to the U.S.

http://aidaonline.niedersachsen.de
Searchable database of emigrants from Hannover, Braunschweig, and
Oldenburg.

www.auswanderer-bw.de/
Searchable database of emigrants from the former states of Baden,
Württemberg, and Hohenzollern.

www.castlegarden.org
Covers U.S. immigration 1820–1913.

www.dad-recherche.de/hmb/index.html
German emigrants database.

www.ellisisland.org
Covers U.S. immigration 1892–1924.

www.lippe-auswanderer.de/
Searchable database of emigrants from Lippe to U.S.

www.passengerlists.de
Contains Bremen passenger lists 1920–1939.

www.stevemorse.org
Provides alternate ways of searching passenger lists and other databases.

Maps and Gazetteers
http://christoph.stoepel.net/geogen/en/Default.aspz
German and Austrian surname distribution maps.

www.falk.de/routenplaner
Online maps in German.

www.hgis-germany.de/
Gazetteer of German historical jurisdictions for each locality.

www.ieg-maps.uni-mainz.de/
Historical maps of Germany.

www.kartenmeister.com
Place names correlated with maps—particularly useful for former eastern areas with multiple place names.

www.library.wisc.edu/etext/ravenstein/
Digitized version of the 1883 Ravenstein *Atlas of the German Empire.*

Phone Directories and Postal Codes
adrressbuch.zlb.de
Berlin Directory for the years 1799–1943.

www.dastelefonbuch.de/
German online phone book.

www.ortschaft.eu/de
German postal codes.

www.teleauskunft.de
German online phone book.

Podcast
www.schmidtgen.com/podcast.php
The German-American Genealogists Podcast.

Religious Groups
https://archive.org/details/brethrendigitalarchives
Church of the Brethren Digital Archive.

www.archives.cg68.fr/
Haut-Rhin Alsatian church records.

www.its-arolsen.org
A center for documentation, information, and research on Nazi persecution, forced labor, and the Holocaust—has 50 million reference cards for 17.5 million individuals.

www.bundesarchiv.de/gedenkbuch/directory.html.en
Searchable list of about 130,000 people from West Germany and Berlin who died in the Holocaust.

http:/etat-civil.bas-rhin.fr/adeloch/index.php
Bas-Rhin Alsatian church records.

www.kirchenbuchportal.de/
New portal for German church records.

https://www2.landesarchiv-bw.de/
Digital copies of Jewish records held by Landesarchiv in Stuttgart.

http://matricula-online.edu
Digitized German and Austrian religious records.

CHAPTER 12: CONTINUATION

This is usually the part of the book where the author melds together everything he has said in all previous pages and writes the magic word CONCLUSION. In a book about searching for your German roots (or any other roots) this cannot be written. Unless you are unbelievably lucky there will never be a conclusion, no end to the road, no finish to the story—there will always be gaps to be filled, questions to be answered. You may have traced your family back 500 years, but in one generation you may have a wife's first name but not her surname, in another you may have dates of baptisms and burials but no date (except an approximate one) for a marriage. These gaps will not mean your proven descent is incomplete, but they will bother you over the years, and you will keep on trying a new approach, thinking up a brilliant idea to solve the problem.

Anyway, do you really ever want to say FINISH? What would you do with your time then? If you started with your father's family, you can now try your mother's. You have grandparents to work on, and great-grandparents too. The possibilities are endless. You can even take on the mammoth project of tracing every living relative!

Apart from the dull parade of "vital events" that make up your family tree, your search will bring you excitement and romance. You will have the thrill of the chase as, step-by-step, you go further back into history. You will have those magic moments when you open a long-awaited letter from Bavaria to find you have gone back another generation. You will find moments of intimacy in old letters and diaries. You may discover touching tributes to one of your ancestors—like one of my wife's Copland forebears who had these wonderful words inscribed on the tombstone of his parents:

> If all those who well knew and could record his integrity, public spirit, and benevolence, and her amiable manners and worth, had been immortal, this memorial need not have been inscribed by their eldest son, William Copland of Colliston. A.D. 1808.

As you trace your family back you will want to know much more about the work they did, the clothes they wore, the houses they lived in, the area in which they were born. You can find all this in local history books, old newspapers, books on sociology, and so on. I found out many things about my sheep-farming ancestors. I know the breed they raised on the high fells above the ancestral valley of Swindale—Herdwicks; I know when they took their sheep to market in Kendal—every Wednesday; I know how much they got for their wool—8 shillings for 14 pounds in 1705; I know when they took the flocks up to the fells for the summer grazing—early in April; I know the food they ate, the clothes they wore, the furniture in their houses. These are the fascinating details that put thick foliage on the bare branches of the family tree.

During all the centuries the Baxters were raising their sheep and their children in their remote, lost dale, my wife's family—the Pearsons— were living some sixty miles away on the upper reaches of the River Tyne. Their life was very different from the Baxters'. Although they, too, had originally been hill farmers, they developed a nose for business and were soon owning lead mines and coal mines and ever-increasing estates. They were lords of the manors of Haltwhistle and Allendale and Hexham—totaling thousands of acres of good farmland and stone quarries and rich summer grazing. They married the daughters of the Earls of Derwentwater and played an active part in the fashionable life of London and Newcastle. They sent one son to manage lead mines in Scotland and another to fight in the lost cause of the Jacobite Rebellion of 1715.

You may discover many similar stories about your ancestors if you dig deep enough. If you are lucky you may well come into possession of family treasures you do not even know about now. As you make contact with distant relatives in the old country—a cousin in the Palatinate, another one in the Black Forest—you will eventually meet, make friendships, and who knows what family heirlooms will be passed on to you?

Perhaps you will find, as I once did, the ruins of an old house once built and occupied by an ancestor. I doubt, however, if any find could be more romantic than mine. Many years ago on a spring morning, just after daybreak, I was poking about in the ruins of an old house called Swindalehead. The silence was total, except for the sound of a few sheep grazing nearby. I found a massive beam that must have been the original support for the bedroom over the living room. Suddenly I noticed some faint carving in the wood. I rubbed away at the dirt and grime, and picked away at the indentation with an old squared nail I found. Finally I could decipher it—JB *IB 1539. I knew who they were! John Baxter and his wife, Isabel Wilkinson, and 1539 was the year of their marriage. I also know that in that year John was nineteen and his wife was eighteen, and they had been given the farm as a wedding present by John's father. Standing in the ruins in the silence and the stillness of that lonely, lovely valley of my ancestors, I could picture the two youngsters setting up house together—John carving the initials in the heavy beam, and Isabel holding firm the chair on which he stood. In that moment all my ancestors crowded around me and all my searching for my roots was worthwhile.

Go forward then—there is still magic in the world, and love and warmth and happiness.

BIBLIOGRAPHY

Note: The Bibliography is a selective one of books found most useful in writing this book. It does not include others written in German, or the many books written about German settlement in states other than Maryland and Pennsylvania, or Canadian provinces other than Ontario and Nova Scotia. For these you should consult your local library or genealogical society.

Anderson, C., and E. Thode. *A Genealogist's Guide to Discovering Your Germanic Ancestors.* Cincinnati: Betterway Books, 2000.

Beidler, James M. *The Family Tree German Genealogy Guide.* Cincinnati: Family Tree Books, 2014.

Bentz, E.M. *If I Can You Can Decipher Germanic Records.* San Diego: E.M. Bentz, 1982; repr. 2006.

Brandt, B., and E.R. Brandt. *Where to Look for Hard-to-find German-Speaking Ancestors in Eastern Europe.* 2nd ed. Baltimore: Genealogical Publishing Co., 1993; repr. 2007.

Brandt, E.R., M. Bellingham, K. Cutkomp, K.E. Frye, P. Lowe, and P. Sternberg. *Germanic Genealogy: A Guide to Worldwide Sources and Migration Patterns.* 3rd ed. St. Paul, Minn.: Germanic Genealogy Society, 2007.

Diffenderffer, F.R. *German Immigration into Pennsylvania.* 1900; repr., Baltimore: Genealogical Publishing Co., 2003.

Egle, W.H. *Early Pennsylvania Land Records.* 1893; repr., Baltimore: Genealogical Publishing Co., 2000.

Eshleman, H.F. *Historic Background and Annals of the Swiss and German Pioneer Settlers of Southeastern Pennsylvania.* 1917; repr., Baltimore: Genealogical Publishing Co., 2006.

Faust, A.B., and G.M. Brumbaugh. *Lists of Swiss Emigrants in the Eighteenth Century to the American Colonies.* 2 vols. 1920–25; repr., Baltimore: Genealogical Publishing Co., 2007.

Genealogical Guide: German Ancestors from East Germany and Eastern Europe. Neustadt (Aisch), Germany: Verlag Degener & Co., 1984.

Glazier, I.A., and P.W. Filby. *Germans to America: Lists of Passengers Arriving at U.S. Ports 1850–1897.* Series I and II, 67 vols. Wilmington, Del.: Scholarly Resources, 1988–2001 (also Lanham, Md.: Scarecrow Press).

Hansen K.M. *Finding Your German Ancestors: A Beginner's Guide.* Provo, Utah: Ancestry, 1999.

Hansen, M.L. *The Atlantic Migration, 1607–1860.* Cambridge, Mass.: Harvard University Press, 1940.

Hocker, E.W. *Genealogical Data Relating to the German Settlers of Pennsylvania and Adjacent Territory.* 1989; repr., Baltimore: Genealogical Publishing Co., 2008.

Irish, D.R. *Pennsylvania German Marriages.* 1982; repr., Baltimore: Genealogical Publishing Co., 2009.

Jensen, L.D. *Genealogical Handbook of German Research.* 2 vols. Pleasant Grove, Utah: L.D. Jensen, 1980.

Jones, G. *German-American Names.* 3rd ed. Baltimore: Genealogical Publishing Co., 2006; repr., 2009.

Jones, HZ, Jr. *Even More Palatine Families.* 3 vols. Camden, Maine: Picton Press, 2002.

_____. *More Palatine Families.* Universal City, Calif.: HZ Jones, 1991.

_____. *The Palatine Families of Ireland.* 2nd ed. Camden, Maine: Picton Press, 1990.

_____. *The Palatine Families of New York 1710.* 2 vols. Universal City, Calif.: HZ Jones, 1985.

Kessler, G. *Die Familiennamen der Juden in Deutschland.* Leipzig: Zentralstelle Für Deutsche Personen- und Familiengeschichte E.V., 1935.

Knittle, W.A. *Early Eighteenth Century Palatine Emigration.* 1937; repr., Baltimore: Genealogical Publishing Co., 2004.

MacWethy, L.D. *The Book of Names Especially Relating to the Early Palatines and the First Settlers in the Mohawk Valley.* 1933; repr., Baltimore: Genealogical Publishing Co., 2007.

Meynen, E. *Bibliography on the Colonial Germans of North America* (originally published as *Bibliography on German Settlements in Colonial North America).* 1937; repr., Baltimore: Genealogical Publishing Co., 1982.

Moltman, G. *Germans to America: 300 Years of Immigration 1683–1983*, Stuttgart, Germany: Institute for Foreign Cultural Relations, 1982.

Nead, D.W. *The Pennsylvania-German in the Settlement of Maryland.* 1914; repr., Baltimore: Genealogical Publishing Co., 2002.

Newman, H.W. *The Flowering of the Maryland Palatinate.* 1961; repr., Baltimore: Genealogical Publishing Co., 2008.

Otterness, Philip. *Becoming German: The 1709 Palatine Migration to New York.* Ithaca, N.Y.: Cornell University Press, 2004.

Pennsylvania German Society. *Pennsylvania German Church Records.* 3 vols. Baltimore: Genealogical Publishing Co., 1983; repr., 2009.

Ribbe, W., and E. Henning. *Taschenbuch für Familiengeschichtsforschung.* 13th ed. Neustadt an der Aisch, Germany: Degener, 2006.

Riemer, S.J., R.P. Minert, and J.A. Anderson. *The German Research Companion.* 3rd ed.. Sacramento, Calif.: Lorelei Press, 2010.

Rupp, I.D. *A Collection of Upwards of Thirty Thousand Names of German . . . Immigrants in Pennsylvania from 1727 to 1776.* 1876; repr., Baltimore: Genealogical Publishing Co., 2006.

Schenk, T., R. Froelke, and I. Bork. *The Wuerttemberg Emigration Index.* 8 vols. Provo, Utah: 1986–2002.

Simmendinger, U. *True and Authentic Register of Persons . . . Who in the Year 1709 . . . Journeyed from Germany to America.* 1934; repr., Baltimore: Genealogical Publishing Co., 1991.

Smith, C.N., and A. Smith. *Encyclopedia of German-American Genealogical Research.* 1976; repr., Baltimore: Genealogical Publishing Co., 2011.

Smith, K. *German Names: A Practical Guide.* Morgantown, Pa.: Masthof Press, 2007.

Staudt, R.W. *Palatine Church Visitations, 1609, Deanery of Kusel.* 1930; repr., Baltimore: Genealogical Publishing Co., 2007.

Steigerwald, J. *Tracing Romania's Heterogeneous German Minority from Its Origins to the Diaspora* (Danubian Swabians). Winona, Minn.: Translation and Interpretation Service, 1985.

Stoever, J.C. *Early Lutheran Baptisms and Marriages in Southeastern Pennsylvania* (originally published as *Records of Rev. John Casper Stoever*). 1896; repr., Baltimore: Genealogical Publishing Co., 2008.

Strassburger, R.B., and W.J. Hinke. *Pennsylvania German Pioneers: A Publication of the Original Lists of Arrivals in the Port of Philadelphia from 1727 to 1808.* 3 vols. 1934; repr., Baltimore: Genealogical Publishing Co., 2002 (vols. I, II), 2014 (vol. III).

Tepper, M. *American Passenger Arrival Records: A Guide to the Records of Immigrants Arriving at American Ports by Sail and Steam.* Updated and enlarged. Baltimore: Genealogical Publishing Co., 1993; repr., 1999.

_____. *Emigrants to Pennsylvania, 1641–1819 . . . from the Pennsylvania Magazine of History and Biography.* 1877–1934; repr., Baltimore: Genealogical Publishing Co., 2009.

_____. *Passenger Arrivals at the Port of Baltimore, 1820–1834.* 1982; repr., Baltimore: Genealogical Publishing Co., 1999.

_____. *Passenger Arrivals at the Port of Philadelphia, 1800–1819.* 1986; repr., Baltimore: Genealogical Publishing Co., 2003.

Thode, Ernest. *Genealogy at a Glance: German Genealogy Research.* Baltimore: Genealogical Publishing Co., 2011.

_____. *German-English Genealogical Dictionary.* Baltimore: Genealogical Publishing Co., 1992; repr., 2008.

_____. *Historic German Newspapers Online.* Baltimore: Genealogical Publishing Co., 2014.

Walker, Mack. *Germany and the Emigration, 1816–1885.* Cambridge, Mass.: Harvard University Press, 1964.

Wright, R.S. III, N.S. Rives, M.J. Kirkham, S.S. Bunting. *Ancestors in German Archives.* 2 vols. Baltimore: Genealogical Publishing Co., 2004; repr., 2010.

_____. *Meyers Orts- und Verkehrs-Lexikon des Deutschen Reichs. With Researcher's Guide and Translations of the Introduction, Instruction for the Use of the Gazetteer, and Abbreviations.* 3 vols. 1912–1913; repr., Baltimore: Genealogical Publishing Co., 2000.

Yoder, D. *Pennsylvania German Immigrants, 1709–1786.* 1984; repr., Baltimore: Genealogical Publishing Co., 2006.

_____. *Rhineland Emigrants.* 1981; repr., Baltimore: Genealogical Publishing Co., 1998.

Zimmerman, G.J. and M. Wolfert. *German Immigrants: Lists of Passengers Bound from Bremen to New York (1847–1867).* 3 vols. Baltimore: Genealogical Publishing Co., 1985–1993.

Canada

Bauman, Salome. *150 Years: First Mennonite Church, 1813–1963* [Kitchener]. Kitchener, Ont.: The Church, 1963.

Baxter, A. *In Search of Your Canadian Roots.* 3rd ed. 1994; repr., Baltimore: Genealogical Publishing Co., 2008.

Bell, W.P. *The Foreign Protestants and the Settlement of Nova Scotia.* Toronto: University of Toronto Press, 1961.

DeMarce, Virginia Easley. *The Settlement of Former German Auxiliary Troops in Canada after the American Revolution.* Sparta, Wisc.: Joy Reisinger, 1984

DesBrisay, M.B. *History of the County of Lunenburg.* 2nd ed. Toronto: 1895.

Eby, E. *A Biographical History of Early Settlers and Their Descendants in Waterloo Township.* 1895; repr., HardPress Publishing, 2012.

Hunsberger, David L, James Hertel, Koni Lattner, and J.W. Fretz. *People Apart: Portrait of a Mennonite World in Waterloo County, Ontario.* St. Jacobs, Ont.: Sand Hills Books, 1978.

Leibbrandt, G. *Little Paradise: The Saga of the German Canadians of Waterloo County, Ontario, 1800–1975.* Kitchener, Ont.: Allprint, 1980.

Moyer, W.G. *This Unique Heritage: The Story of Waterloo County.* Kitchener, Ont.: Radio Station CHYM, 1971.

Punch, T. *Genealogical Research in Nova Scotia.* Halifax: Petheric Press, 1978.

Reaman, G.E. *The Trail of the Black Walnut* [Pennsylvania to Canada]. 1957; repr., Baltimore: Genealogical Publishing Co., 2012.

Uttley, W.V. *A History of Kitchener* [1865–1944]. 1937; repr., Kitchener, Ont.: Wilfred Laurier University Press, 1975.

Note: Three early German newspapers (*Canada Museum, Deutsche Canadier,* and *Berliner Journal*) have been indexed for birth, marriage, and death entries by the Kitchener Public Library.

INDEX

CPSIA information can be obtained at www.ICGtesting.com
Printed in the USA
BVOW08s1123270515

401948BV00006B/19/P